WILLIAMS-SONOMA

MEXICAN

RECIPES AND TEXT
MARILYN TAUSEND

GENERAL EDITOR
CHUCK WILLIAMS

PHOTOGRAPHS
MAREN CARUSO

SIMON & SCHUSTER • **SOURCE**

NEW YORK • LONDON • TORONTO • SYDNEY • SINGAPORE

CONTENTS

SEAFOOD AND POULTRY

PORK, BEEF, AND LAMB

DESSERTS

INTRODUCTION

Mexico has one of the world's most diverse culinary histories. Its earliest inhabitants were sustained for thousands of years by corn and beans, enlivened with ingredients such as squashes, tomatoes, chiles, and chocolate—all native to the New World. With the arrival of the Spanish came the additions of rice, wheat, and citrus fruits, as well as spices from the Far East. When one considers the diverse Mexican landscape—expansive coasts, high mountains, and dense jungles—and the range of ingredients each region offers, it is easy to see how Mexico has developed such a rich culinary heritage.

This book aims to share this richness with you through its recipes, including a long-simmered mole poblano, a simple ceviche, and an innovative chocolate cake flavored with a touch of ancho chile. In addition, informative side notes will help you familiarize yourself with the history of Mexican cooking as well as its techniques and ingredients. I urge you to try these recipes and to bring one of the world's favorite cuisines into your own kitchen.

Chuck Williams

THE CLASSICS

Every part of Mexico has its own regional foods, but there are some dishes that are known throughout the country. Guacamole is served everywhere, as are tamales, chilaquiles, *and enchiladas. There are also some recipes, such as stuffed poblano chiles with walnut sauce, Veracruz-style red snapper, and mole poblano, that are unique to just one region but are so celebrated that they have become classics.* ¡Buen provecho!

GUACAMOLE WITH HOMEMADE TORTILLA CHIPS
10

CEVICHE
13

CHICKEN ENCHILADAS WITH SALSA ROJA
14

CHILAQUILES WITH SALSA VERDE
17

STUFFED POBLANO CHILES WITH WALNUT SAUCE
18

PORK TAMALES WITH RED CHILE SAUCE
20

VERACRUZ-STYLE RED SNAPPER
25

MOLE POBLANO
26

GUACAMOLE WITH HOMEMADE TORTILLA CHIPS

PREPARING AVOCADOS

To test if an avocado is ripe, gently press it; it should give slightly. To fully ripen, place it in a paper bag with a banana. Ethylene gases emitted by the banana will speed the ripening process. To prepare an avocado, halve lengthwise with a knife, cutting around the pit. Rotate the halves to separate. Set the half with the pit on a work surface and, using the heel of the knife blade, strike the pit and twist to draw it out. To remove the flesh, ease a spoon between the flesh and skin, or peel the skin with a knife. Or, while still in the skin, cut the flesh into cubes (see recipe method, page 13).

To make the chips, stack the tortillas in 6 piles of 3 tortillas each. Using a sharp knife, cut each pile into 4–6 wedges. Spread the wedges out in a single layer, cover with a heavy kitchen towel to prevent them from curling, and let dry out for several hours.

Preheat the oven to 250°F (120°C). Pour the oil to a depth of at least 1 inch (2.5 cm) into a deep, heavy frying pan and heat over medium-high heat to 375°F (190°C) on a deep-frying thermometer, or until a piece of tortilla dropped into the oil quickly becomes crisp (see Note). Add a handful of the wedges and fry, tossing them with a slotted spoon, until they are crisp and lightly golden, about 30 seconds. Do not let them darken, or they will be bitter. Using the slotted spoon, transfer to paper towels to drain. Repeat with the remaining wedges. Season them with sea salt, if desired, while still warm, and keep warm in the oven until all are fried.

To make the guacamole, in a *molcajete* or a bowl, mash 4 tablespoons (1½ oz/45 g) of the onion, the chiles, and the garlic (if using) with a pestle or fork to form a coarse paste. Add the avocado and mash until well incorporated. Stir in all but 2 tablespoons of the tomato and all of the cilantro and lime juice. Season to taste with sea salt. Let stand for a few minutes before serving. Sprinkle the guacamole with the remaining onion and tomato and serve accompanied with the warm tortilla chips.

Note: Do not let the temperature of the oil rise above 375°F (190°C). If it reaches 400°F (200°C) or more, it may start to smoke, then burst into flame.

Serving Tip: You may also serve the guacamole with jicama sticks. To prepare, peel away the skin from a 1-lb (500-g) jicama. Halve lengthwise, then cut each half into slices ½ inch (12 mm) thick. Cut the slices into sticks ½ inch wide and sprinkle with fresh lime juice.

MAKES 2½ CUPS (20 OZ/625 G), OR 8 APPETIZER SERVINGS

FOR THE TORTILLA CHIPS:

18 white corn tortillas, the thinnest possible, 4–6 inches (10–15 cm) in diameter

Canola or safflower oil for deep-frying

Sea salt (optional)

FOR THE GUACAMOLE:

6 tablespoons (2 oz/60 g) finely chopped white onion

2 serrano chiles, seeded (page 39) and finely chopped

1 clove garlic, minced (optional)

2 ripe Hass avocados, halved, pitted, and peeled *(far left)*

1 large, ripe tomato, finely chopped

¼ cup (¼ oz/7 g) lightly packed fresh cilantro (fresh coriander) leaves, finely chopped

1 tablespoon fresh lime juice

Sea salt

CEVICHE

¾ lb (375 g) salmon fillet

½ lb (250 g) bay scallops or sea scallops, cut into ½-inch (12-mm) cubes

⅓ white onion, cut into ¼-inch (6-mm) dice

1 cup (8 fl oz/250 ml) fresh lime juice

½ cup (4 fl oz/125 ml) fresh orange juice

4 ripe plum (Roma) tomatoes or 1 large ripe tomato, cut into ¼-inch (6-mm) dice

3 serrano or jalapeño chiles, minced

¼ cup (¼ oz/7 g) loosely packed fresh cilantro (fresh coriander) leaves, finely chopped, plus whole leaves for garnish

3 tablespoons extra-virgin olive oil

Sea salt

1 ripe Hass avocado

Tortilla chips, homemade (page 10) or purchased

Remove the skin from the salmon fillet if it is still intact and run your fingers over the fillet to check for and remove any embedded bones, using tweezers if necessary. Cut the fish into ½-inch (12-mm) cubes and place in a large glass or stainless-steel bowl. Add the scallops, onion, and lime and orange juices and toss to mix well. Cover and refrigerate until the fish is opaque throughout when a piece is sliced open, about 4 hours.

Just before serving, drain off and discard the excess juice from the bowl. Add the tomatoes, chiles, chopped cilantro, and olive oil and mix well. Season with ½ teaspoon sea salt.

Halve the avocado and remove the pit (page 10). Using a knife, and holding one avocado half, flesh side up, cut lengthwise through the flesh to make slices ¼ inch (6 mm) thick, being careful not to cut through the skin. Then make crosswise cuts ¼ inch thick, to create cubes. Using a large spoon, scoop the cubes from the skin. Repeat with the remaining half. Add the avocado cubes to the fish mixture and toss gently.

Divide the ceviche among small clear-glass bowls, wineglasses, or martini glasses. Garnish each serving with cilantro leaves. Serve with the tortilla chips.

Serving Tip: You can omit the tortilla chips and instead serve the ceviche tostada-style. Follow the instructions on page 40 for frying tortillas. Place a fried tortilla on each individual plate and mound the ceviche on top.

MAKES 6 APPETIZER SERVINGS

ABOUT CEVICHE
One of the simplest ways to serve seafood, ceviche is bite-sized pieces of very fresh raw fish and/or shellfish "cooked" by the acid in fresh citrus juice, rather than by heat. The origin of ceviche remains a subject of debate; however, its first recorded appearance in Mexico was in Acapulco in the sixteenth century. The most common theory is that the recipe arrived with long-distance fishermen from northern Chile and Peru. Other experts believe that it arrived on the galleons that plied the waters between Manila and Acapulco.

CHICKEN ENCHILADAS WITH SALSA ROJA

Make the *salsa roja*, or red chile sauce, by tearing the chiles into large pieces. Put them in a heatproof bowl and add boiling water to cover. Weight the chiles down with a plate and let soak until soft, about 15 minutes. Drain the chiles. In batches, in a blender, process the chiles, tomatoes with juice, chopped onion, garlic, and oregano until smooth, adding ½ cup (4 fl oz/125 ml) or more of the chicken stock as needed to achieve a very smooth consistency.

Preheat the oven to 325°F (165°C). In a frying pan over medium heat, heat 1 tablespoon of the oil until it is shimmering but not smoking. Pour in the chile sauce and cook, stirring, until quite thick, about 2 minutes. Add the remaining chicken stock and cook, stirring frequently, until thick, about 5 minutes. Taste and adjust the seasoning with sea salt. Remove from the heat and set aside; keep warm. Spoon a thin layer of the chile sauce on the bottom of a 9-by-13-inch (23-by-33-cm) baking dish and keep warm.

In a frying pan over medium heat, heat the remaining 3 tablespoons oil until sizzling hot. Using tongs and a spatula, very quickly drag the tortillas one at a time through the oil to soften them on both sides. Pat dry with paper towels. Dip a softened tortilla into the warm sauce in the frying pan and then lay it on a plate. Spread 1 heaping tablespoon of the shredded chicken near the edge closest to you, roll up the tortilla, and place, seam side down, in the prepared baking dish. Repeat with the remaining tortillas and chicken, arranging the rolled tortillas side by side in the dish. When the dish is filled, spoon the remaining chile sauce evenly over the tortillas. Bake the enchiladas until heated through, about 5 minutes. Divide the enchiladas among warmed individual plates and top with the *crema*, onion rings, and radishes. Serve at once, as the enchiladas will quickly become soggy.

MAKES 12 ENCHILADAS, OR 5 OR 6 SERVINGS

ANCHO CHILES

The ancho, the dried form of the fresh poblano chile, is used extensively in sauces and moles and for stuffing. *Ancho* means "wide" in Spanish, and the broad shoulders (at least 2 inches/5 cm wide) of this dark burgundy chile are what distinguish it from most of its dried cousins. The mulato chile looks similar, but its skin is almost black when the chile is held up to the light. The ancho and mulato should not be used interchangeably, as the ancho has a rather sweet, chocolaty, fruity flavor, and the mulato is not sweet at all.

10 ancho chiles, seeded (page 108)

1 can (14½ oz/455 g) diced tomatoes, with juice

½ white onion, coarsely chopped, plus 1 small white onion, thinly sliced and separated into rings

6 cloves garlic

1 teaspoon dried oregano, preferably Mexican

1½ cups (12 fl oz/375 ml) chicken stock (page 110) or prepared low-sodium broth

4 tablespoons (2 fl oz/60 ml) canola or safflower oil

Sea salt

12 white corn tortillas, about 6 inches (15 cm) in diameter

2 cups (12 oz/375 g) coarsely shredded poached (page 113) or leftover roasted chicken

½ cup (4 fl oz/125 ml) *crema* (page 51)

6 radishes, trimmed and thinly sliced

14

CHILAQUILES WITH SALSA VERDE

1 lb (500 g) tomatillos, husked and rinsed *(far right)*

4 serrano chiles

2 cloves garlic

½ white onion, coarsely chopped, plus 1 or more thin white onion slices, separated into rings

1 tablespoon canola or safflower oil

Sea salt

½ lb (250 g) thick tortilla chips, homemade (page 10) or purchased (about 8 cups)

¼ cup (⅓ oz/10 g) coarsely chopped fresh cilantro (fresh coriander)

1 cup (8 fl oz/250 ml) *crema* (page 51)

½ cup (2½ oz/75 g) crumbled *queso fresco* (page 115) or mild feta cheese

Put the tomatillos in a small saucepan and add water to barely cover. Bring to a simmer over medium heat and cook until the tomatillos begin to soften, about 5 minutes. Add the chiles and garlic and continue cooking until the tomatillos are soft, about 5 minutes longer. Remove from the heat.

Using a slotted spoon, transfer the tomatillos, chiles, and garlic to a blender; reserve the cooking liquid. Add the chopped onion and ½ cup (4 fl oz/125 ml) of the cooking liquid to the blender and process until well blended, leaving some texture.

In a large frying pan or *cazuela* over medium-high heat, heat the oil until it is shimmering but not smoking. Pour in the tomatillo mixture all at once and stir vigorously. Stir in an additional ½ cup of the reserved cooking liquid, along with ½ teaspoon sea salt, reduce the heat to low, and cook, uncovered, until the sauce thickens, about 10 minutes. Add more liquid if necessary.

Just before serving, carefully stir the tortilla chips and cilantro into the sauce and continue cooking until softened but not mushy, about 5 minutes. Taste and adjust the seasoning with sea salt.

Scoop the mixture into a warmed serving dish or onto warmed individual plates. To garnish, spoon on the *crema* and scatter the onion rings and cheese on top.

Make-Ahead Tip: The sauce can be made up to 3 days in advance. Let cool, cover, and refrigerate, then reheat over medium-low heat, thinning with water if necessary.

Serving Tip: This recipe makes a wonderful breakfast dish for company or can be served as a light supper.

MAKES 4 SERVINGS

TOMATILLOS

Despite its appearance, a tomatillo is not a type of green tomato, although both are members of the nightshade family. The tomatillo is covered with a parchmentlike calyx that, when removed, reveals a fruit that looks like a firm green or purplish cherry tomato. The fruits, which have a unique texture and tart flavor, are the basis for many cooked sauces, *pipianes,* and moles, and are occasionally used raw in salsas. Carefully rinse off the sticky residue that covers the skin before using.

STUFFED POBLANO CHILES WITH WALNUT SAUCE

WALNUT SAUCE

A celebrated version of *chiles rellenos*, these stuffed chiles are usually made in early autumn when a new crop of milky-white walnuts is available. To make the sauce, in a blender, process 2 cups (8 oz/250 g) walnuts; 2 cups (1 lb/500 g) sour cream; 12 oz (375 g) cream cheese, at room temperature; and 1 cup (8 fl oz/250 ml) whole milk. Add 1 teaspoon sea salt, ¼ teaspoon ground cinnamon, and ⅛ teaspoon freshly grated nutmeg and purée until the mixture is smooth. Taste and stir in ½ teaspoon sugar, if needed. Cover and refrigerate to chill well.

To make the *picadillo*, in a large, heavy frying pan or Dutch oven over medium-high heat, heat the oil until it shimmers. Add the onion and sauté until lightly colored, about 1 minute. Stir in the pork and cook until it is no longer pink and just starts to brown, about 6 minutes. Add the tomatoes and juice and cook, uncovered, until the meat is thoroughly cooked and tender, 10–15 minutes. Reduce the heat to low and add the apple, pear, plantain, almonds, raisins, and *acitrón*. Stir gently, then add the cinnamon, cloves, and ½ teaspoon sea salt, or more to taste. (It may need more salt than you think.) Continue to cook, stirring from time to time, until most of the moisture has evaporated, about 5 minutes. Remove from the heat.

Stuff the chiles with the *picadillo* until plump and just barely closed. Place on a serving platter or individual plates, cover with the chilled walnut sauce, sprinkle with the pomegranate seeds, and garnish with the parsley. Serve at once.

Notes: This renowned dish is called chiles en nogada *in Mexico. It is resplendent with the red, green, and white colors of the Mexican flag and was created by the early convent nuns in Puebla in honor of a visit by a special guest. This recipe is always served around Independence Day, September 15, when the new crop of walnuts is ready and pomegranates are ripe. When buying the poblanos, buy a couple extra in case you tear any when you are peeling them.*

Make-Ahead Tip: The picadillo, *a well-seasoned mixture of minced meat and fruit, can be made up to 1 day in advance. Let cool, cover, and refrigerate, then reheat over medium-low heat.*

MAKES 12 STUFFED CHILES; OR 6–12 SERVINGS

FOR THE PICADILLO:

¼ cup (2 fl oz/60 ml) canola or safflower oil

½ cup (2½ oz/75 g) finely chopped white onion

2 lb (1 kg) lean pork loin, finely chopped

1 can (28 oz/875 g) chopped tomatoes, with juice

⅔ cup (4 oz/125 g) *each* peeled and finely cubed apple, pear, and ripe plantain (page 115)

⅓ cup (1½ oz/45 g) chopped blanched almonds

⅓ cup (2 oz/60 g) raisins, chopped

⅓ cup (2 oz/60 g) finely cubed *acitrón* (page 113) or candied pineapple

½ teaspoon ground cinnamon

⅛ teaspoon ground cloves

Sea salt

12 large poblano chiles, roasted, peeled, and seeded, with stem intact (page 106; see Notes)

Walnut Sauce *(far left)*

Pomegranate seeds and fresh flat-leaf (Italian) parsley sprigs for garnish

PORK TAMALES WITH RED CHILE SAUCE

WRAPPING TAMALES

In Spanish, the singular of "tamales" is *tamal*. To wrap a *tamal*, lay a husk in one palm, with the pointed end on your wrist. Spread a generous tablespoon of the dough thinly in the center of the upper half and 4 inches (10 cm) down the husk, leaving a margin on all sides. Place a few pieces of the meat and some sauce down the center of the dough, then fold the long edges of the husk over the filling, overlapping them and forming a narrow *tamal*. Bring up the pointed end of the husk until it is even with the cut end. Tie the end with a husk strip to secure.

Put the pork, garlic, peppercorns, and 1 teaspoon sea salt in a large saucepan or Dutch oven. Add 4 cups (32 fl oz/1 l) water or as needed to cover. Bring to a low boil over medium-high heat, skimming off any foam that forms on the surface. Reduce the heat to low, cover, and simmer the pork until tender, about 45 minutes. Remove from the heat and let the pork cool in the broth. Using a slotted spoon, transfer the pork to a bowl and set aside. Spoon off as much fat from the surface of the broth as possible; there should be 3 cups (24 fl oz/750 ml) broth remaining. If not, add water to equal that amount.

In a small bowl, stir together the ground chiles and cumin and then stir in ½ cup (4 fl oz/125 ml) of the broth to make a thin paste. Stir the chile paste back into the broth, mixing well.

In a large, dry frying pan over low heat, toast the flour, stirring constantly, for a few seconds, just until it starts to brown. Drizzle in enough oil to saturate the flour and continue to stir until the mixture is a rich brown. Stirring constantly, gradually add the chile broth, raise the heat to medium, and cook, stirring frequently, until the sauce thickens and no lumps remain, about 3 minutes. Add the sugar, oregano, and sea salt to taste. Pour half of the sauce into the pork and broth and set aside. Cover the remaining sauce in the pan with plastic wrap pressed directly onto the surface; set aside. Rinse the corn husks and then soak in hot water to cover until pliable, about 15 minutes.

In a large bowl, stir together the *masa harina*, chile powder, baking powder, and 1 tablespoon sea salt. Stir in enough lukewarm water, 3–4 cups (24–32 oz/750 ml–1 l), to make a moist batter. In a small bowl using an electric mixer, beat the lard until creamy, at least 5 minutes. Add to the *masa harina* mixture and continue beating until the mixture is quite light and spreadable, about 5 minutes longer, adding up to ⅓ cup (3 fl oz/80 ml) more water if too dry. Taste and adjust the seasoning with sea salt.

1 lb (500 g) boneless pork butt or shoulder, cut into ½-inch (12-mm) cubes

3 cloves garlic

4 peppercorns

Sea salt

2 ancho chiles, toasted and seeded (page 108), then finely ground (page 114)

2 árbol chiles, toasted and seeded (page 108), then finely ground (page 114)

¼ teaspoon ground cumin

½ cup (2½ oz/75 g) all-purpose (plain) flour

About 2 tablespoons canola or safflower oil

1 teaspoon sugar

½ teaspoon dried oregano, preferably Mexican

50 dried corn husks

4 cups (2½ lb/1.25 kg) *masa harina* (page 35)

2 teaspoons pure chile powder (page 113)

1½ teaspoons baking powder

1–1½ cups (8–12 oz/ 250–375 g) fresh pork lard (page 114) or solid vegetable shortening, at room temperature

Drain the husks and pat dry. Set aside the 30 best husks in a pile for making the tamales. Use the remaining, more ragged husks for lining the steamer and for making ties. Fill the bottom of a large pot with water to a depth of about 3 inches (7.5 cm). Add a clean coin to the pot; when the water boils, the coin will rattle, letting you know that there is still enough water for steaming. Place a steamer basket or circular cake cooling rack in the pot, making certain that the water level is not touching the bottom of the basket or rack. (You may need to set the rack on 4 inverted, heatproof custard cups or ramekins.)

Cover the bottom of the steamer basket or rack with some of the ragged corn husks and put an inverted metal funnel, or an empty tuna fish can with the top and bottom removed, on top. Line up the good corn husks, the dough, and the filling. Tear some of the ragged husks into narrow strips to use as ties. Prepare the tamales *(far left)* and arrange in the pot for steaming *(right)*. Cover the tamales with more ragged corn husks, a clean kitchen towel, and a layer of plastic wrap so no steam escapes. Cover with a tight lid, bring to a low boil over medium-high heat, and steam without opening. (If at any time you do not hear the coin rattling in the pot, take out the steamer basket and pour in more hot water.) After 50 minutes, take out a *tamal*, let it rest for several minutes, and then open it. It is done if the dough easily pulls away from the husk. If not, turn off the heat and let steam for another 10 minutes.

When the tamales are ready, remove from the pot and let sit for several minutes. Reheat the reserved sauce over low heat, adding more water if it is too thick. Remove the corn husks from the tamales, place 2 or 3 tamales on each individual plate, and pour some of the hot sauce over the top. Serve at once.

MAKES 30 TAMALES. OR 10–15 SERVINGS

(Photograph appears on following page.)

21

STEAMING TAMALES

To steam tamales, you will need a steamer basket or circular rack that fits in the bottom of a large pot, as well as an inverted metal funnel or an empty tuna fish can with the top and bottom removed. Together, these tools will allow you to perfectly steam the tamales without letting them come into contact with the water in the bottom of the pan. To arrange the tamales for steaming, starting in the center and working circularly, place each *tamal,* pointed end up and at a slightly vertical angle, in the steamer, with the first layer supported by the funnel or can in the center.

VERACRUZ-STYLE RED SNAPPER

1 whole red snapper, 3–3½ lb (1.5–1.75 kg), scaled and cleaned, with head on, or 6 red snapper fillets, about 5–6 oz (155–185 g) each

8 large cloves garlic

2 teaspoons fresh lime juice

Sea salt

FOR THE SAUCE:

¼ cup (2 fl oz/60 ml) olive oil

1 large white onion, thinly sliced

4 large cloves garlic, minced

3 lb (1.5 kg) ripe tomatoes, roasted and peeled (page 108), then finely chopped

20 small green pimiento-stuffed olives, each cut lengthwise into 4 slices

½ cup (¾ oz/20 g) coarsely chopped fresh flat-leaf (Italian) parsley leaves

3 bay leaves

3 pickled jalapeño chiles, cut lengthwise into strips, with 1 tablespoon pickling liquid

1 tablespoon capers

½ teaspoon *each* dried oregano, marjoram, and thyme, or 4 fresh sprigs *each*

Sea salt and freshly ground pepper

If using a whole fish, rinse it inside and out and pat dry. Prick through the skin of the fish with the tip of a knife every few inches on both sides. If using fillets, omit piercing. Using a mortar and pestle, mash the garlic to a paste and transfer it to a small bowl, or squeeze it through a garlic press. Add the lime juice and ½ teaspoon sea salt and mix well. If using a whole fish, rub the inside and outside of the fish with the garlic mixture. If using fillets, rub the paste over both sides of each fillet. Wrap the fish in plastic wrap and marinate in the refrigerator for at least 30 minutes or for up to 2 hours, turning the fish occasionally for even coating.

Preheat the oven to 350°F (180°C). To make the sauce, in a large, heavy frying pan over medium heat, heat the olive oil. Add the onion and sauté until soft, about 4 minutes. Add the garlic and continue cooking until golden, 1–2 minutes. Raise the heat to medium-high, add the tomatoes, and continue cooking, stirring frequently, until the sauce thickens, 5–7 minutes. Reduce the heat to low and stir in the olives, parsley, bay leaves, chiles and pickling liquid, and capers. Add the oregano, marjoram, thyme, and pepper to taste and simmer, stirring occasionally, until the flavors are well blended, 8–10 minutes. Season to taste with sea salt.

Lightly oil a large glass or ceramic baking dish. Unwrap the fish, place it in the dish, and spoon the sauce evenly over the top, discarding the bay leaves. Bake, basting occasionally with the sauce, just until the flesh is opaque throughout when tested in the thickest part, about 45 minutes for a whole fish or 8–10 minutes for fillets. Do not to overcook the fish. Serve directly from the baking dish or, using 2 spatulas, carefully transfer to a warmed platter.

Serving Tips: Garnish with whole pitted green olives, fresh flat-leaf (Italian) parsley sprigs, whole pickled jalapeño and güero chiles, and/or fresh bay leaves. Accompany with White Rice (page 110).

MAKES 6 SERVINGS

VERACRUZ CUISINE

Veracruz is a raucous port city on the Gulf of Mexico where seafood of all sorts is eaten morning, noon, and long into the night. The most famous of all of the city's dishes combines the silvery-tinged, deep-red-skinned snapper caught in local waters with an equally colorful sauce. When a dish is described as *a la Veracruzana,* it refers to this thick, herby tomato sauce studded with olives and capers that originated in Spain. Pickled light yellow güero, or blond, chiles are always included as a garnish for both flavor and color.

MOLE POBLANO

MOLES

Mole poblano, one of the wonders of the Mexican culinary world, is reserved for special celebrations. Other moles—a word meaning "mixture" or "sauce"—are found throughout most of Mexico, but this nearly black, voluptuous dish, said to have originated in the tile-clad kitchen of the Convent of Santa Rosa in Puebla, epitomizes the culinary union of the Spanish and Mexican worlds. The original recipe mixed together over one hundred ingredients from both continents, along with exotic spices from Asia, to create the complex blend.

In a heavy frying pan over medium heat, melt 4 tablespoons of the lard. Add several chile pieces at a time and fry briefly on both sides just until they begin to change color, about 20 seconds. Lift out with tongs, draining off excess fat, and put in a bowl. When all the chiles are fried, cover them with very hot water, weight them down with a plate, and let soak until soft, about 20 minutes.

Add 1 tablespoon lard to the same pan, place over medium heat, and fry the raisins until they are plump, about 20 seconds. Scoop out with a slotted spoon, draining off excess fat, and put in a bowl. Fry the almonds in the same fat until lightly brown, about 5 minutes. Scoop out with the spoon, again draining off as much fat as possible, and add to the raisins. Add the plantain slices to the pan and fry, turning as needed, until golden, about 5 minutes. Transfer to paper towels to drain. Add more lard, if necessary, and fry the bread slice until golden and crisp, about 1 minute per side. Transfer to paper towels. Add the tortilla pieces and fry until just crisp, about 45 seconds. Drain on paper towels. Add the plantain, bread, and tortilla pieces to the nuts and raisins.

In a small, dry frying pan over medium heat, toast the sesame seeds, stirring constantly, until golden, about 2 minutes. Set aside 2 tablespoons for garnish and pour the rest into a small bowl. In the same pan, toast the ancho chile seeds over medium heat for 1 minute and add them to the sesame seeds. Toast the pumpkin seeds over medium heat for about 30 seconds and add to the rest of the seeds. Using the same pan, toast the aniseeds, coriander seeds, cloves, and cinnamon bark over medium heat, shaking the pan constantly, until very aromatic, just a few seconds. Add to the bowl holding the seeds and stir to mix. In small batches, grind the seed mixture in a spice grinder until pulverized. Set aside.

Remove the chiles from the water, reserving the water. In small batches, put the chiles and a little of the soaking water in a blender and process until very smooth.

3/4 cup (6 oz/180 g) fresh pork lard (page 114) or 3/4 cup (6 fl oz/180 ml) canola oil

6 ancho chiles, seeded (page 108) and torn into large pieces, with 1 tablespoon seeds reserved

4 mulato chiles, seeded (page 108) and torn into large pieces

3 pasilla chiles, seeded (page 108) and torn into large pieces

1/4 cup (1 1/2 oz/45 g) raisins

1/4 cup (1 1/2 oz/45 g) almonds

1/4 plantain (page 115), very soft and ripe, peeled and sliced

1 thick slice day-old French bread or French roll

1 day-old corn tortilla, broken into large pieces

1/4 cup (3/4 oz/20 g) sesame seeds

1/4 cup (1 1/4 oz/37 g) raw hulled green pumpkin seeds

1/2 teaspoon aniseeds

1/2 teaspoon coriander seeds

2 whole cloves

2-inch (5-cm) piece true cinnamon bark (page 85)

10–12 cups (2½–3 qt/ 2.5–3 l) chicken or turkey stock (page 110) or prepared low-sodium broth

4 tomatoes, about 1 lb (500 g) total weight, roasted (page 108)

½ white onion, sliced and roasted (page 65)

3 cloves garlic, roasted (page 65)

½–1 tablet (1½–3 oz/ 45–90 g) Mexican chocolate, broken into small pieces

1 tablespoon sugar, if needed

Sea salt

FOR THE TURKEY:

3–4 lb (1.5–2 kg) boneless turkey breast halves with skin on

3 cups (24 fl oz/750 ml) chicken or turkey stock (page 110) or prepared low-sodium broth

½ white onion, thickly sliced

2 cloves garlic

Sea salt

Place a Dutch oven large enough to hold 5 qt (5 l) or a large *cazuela* over high heat, add 6 tablespoons (3 oz/90 g) lard, and heat until very hot and shimmering. Using a wooden spoon, press the chile mixture through a medium-mesh sieve held over the pan. Discard the solids. Fry, stirring constantly, until thick and the pan bottom is visible when scraped, 6–8 minutes. Reduce the heat to low, stir in 6 cups (48 fl oz/1.5 l) of the stock, and keep at a simmer.

In a blender, in 3 or 4 batches, process the roasted tomatoes, onion, and garlic, along with the fried raisins, almonds, plantain, bread, and tortilla, adding 1 cup (8 fl oz/250 ml) of the stock to each batch, until thoroughly blended. Stir into the chile mixture, along with the reserved ground seeds and spices. Continue cooking over low heat, stirring often, for 30 minutes longer.

Add half of the chocolate to the mole along with the sugar and sea salt to taste. Continue simmering for 20 minutes longer, stirring frequently and scraping the pan bottom, adding more stock if it becomes too thick. Taste again for salt and sugar, and if you want a stronger chocolate flavor, add the rest of the chocolate (it should add only a shadow of bitterness). Continue cooking until pools of oil form on the surface, at least 1 hour longer. For the best flavor, let cool, then cover and refrigerate overnight. Reheat the next day.

About 1½ hours before serving, cook the turkey. Put the turkey, stock, onion, garlic, and 1½ teaspoons sea salt in a Dutch oven. Add just enough water to cover the turkey. Cook over high heat until boiling, then reduce the heat to very low. Cook until the juices run clear when the turkey is pierced at the thickest part with a fork, about 15 minutes. Remove the turkey and let stand until cool enough to handle. Cut into slices ½ inch (12 mm) thick and spoon the mole over and around the turkey, sprinkle with the reserved sesame seeds, and serve.

MAKES 8 SERVINGS

(Photograph appears on following page.)

MEXICAN CHOCOLATE
Chocolate, made from the seeds of the cacao tree, a native of Mexico, was a sacred drink of the Maya, who sometimes flavored it with chile or mixed it with maize. Even its botanical genus, *Theobroma*, means "food of the gods." Thus, it is not surprising that when the nuns created the now-famous mole poblano for some special visitors, they added chocolate to the pot. Other moles contain wisps of chocolate, but it is not always an essential ingredient. Today, so-called Mexican chocolate, a mixture of ground cacao, sugar, cinnamon, and sometimes almonds, is sold in large tablets.

LITTLE BITES AND SNACKS

"Little whims" and "sudden cravings" are both phrases used to describe antojitos, *the little bites and snacks in this chapter. These are the foods of the street—in Guadalajara, you can find* flautas *sold in the busy markets, while in Baja, you will find stands where chunks of fresh fish are being made into tacos. One seldom finds a street corner without someone selling food, as snacking is a characteristic way of eating in Mexico.*

FISH TACOS

SALSA FRESCA

This chunky fresh salsa is the reigning condiment of Mexico. It also goes by the names of *salsa mexicana* or *pico de gallo* in some regions. In a bowl, toss together 1 lb (500 g) ripe tomatoes, cut into ¼-inch (6-mm) pieces; ¼ cup (1½ oz/ 45 g) finely chopped white onion; ¼ cup (⅓ oz/10 g) loosely packed chopped fresh cilantro (fresh coriander); 3 serrano or jalapeño chiles, seeded (page 39) and finely chopped; and 2 teaspoons fresh lime juice. Season to taste with sea salt. Cover and let stand for 10–15 minutes to allow the flavors to mingle. Makes about 2 cups (16 fl oz/500 ml).

To make the batter, in a bowl, stir together the flour, garlic salt, and ground chile. Pour in the beer, whisking to make a smooth batter. Cover and let stand for up to 1 hour. Meanwhile, make the creamy salsa: In a small bowl, stir together the mayonnaise, ketchup, and yogurt until blended. Set aside. To make the tacos, remove the skin from the fish fillet if it is still intact and run your fingers over the fillet to check for and remove any embedded bones, using tweezers if necessary. Cut the fish into 8 strips, each 3–4 inches (7.5–10 cm) long and ¾ inch (2 cm) wide, and place in a nonaluminum bowl. Sprinkle with the lime juice, garlic salt, and ground chile and toss to mix. Let marinate at room temperature for 10 minutes. Pour the oil to a depth of 1 inch (2.5 cm) into a deep-frying pan and heat to 375°F (190°C) on a deep-frying thermometer (see Note, page 10). This may take up to 5 minutes.

Meanwhile, heat a *comal*, griddle, or heavy frying pan over medium heat. When it is hot, stack 2 or 3 tortillas on the heated surface and leave for a few seconds. Flip the tortillas, rotating them every second or so until all are hot. Wrap in a dry kitchen towel and repeat with the remaining tortillas. They should keep warm for 10 minutes. If they are to be held longer, wrap a damp towel around the dry towel and place the packet in a 200°F (95°C) oven.

Pat the fish strips dry with paper towels. One at a time, dip a strip into the batter, allowing the excess to drip off, and slip into the hot oil. Do not allow the pieces to touch. Fry until the strips are crisp and golden, about 7 minutes. Using a slotted spatula, transfer to paper towels to drain. When all are fried, transfer to a warmed serving plate. Put the *salsa fresca*, cabbage, and limes in separate small bowls and set on the table along with the fish, creamy salsa, tortillas, and hot-pepper sauce. Let the diners make their own tacos, wrapping the fish in a tortilla and adding the other items.

MAKES 8 TACOS, OR 4 SERVINGS

FOR THE BATTER:

1 cup (5 oz/155 g) all-purpose (plain) flour

1 teaspoon garlic salt

½ teaspoon ground árbol chile (page 114) or cayenne pepper

1 cup (8 fl oz/250 ml) beer, preferably dark, or milk, at room temperature

FOR THE CREAMY SALSA:

⅓ cup (3 fl oz/80 ml) mayonnaise

⅓ cup (3 oz/90 g) ketchup

⅓ cup (3 oz/90 g) plain yogurt

¾ lb (375 g) red snapper or sea bass fillet

1 teaspoon fresh lime juice

½ teaspoon garlic salt

¼ teaspoon ground árbol chile or cayenne pepper

Canola oil for deep-frying

8 white corn tortillas, about 6 inches (15 cm) in diameter

Salsa Fresca *(far left),* finely shredded cabbage, 8 lime quarters, and bottled hot-pepper sauce for serving

QUESADILLAS WITH POBLANO CHILES

FOR THE TORTILLAS:

2 cups *masa harina*

1¼ cups (10 fl oz/310 ml) plus 2 tablespoons warm water

¼ teaspoon sea salt

FOR THE FILLING:

1 tablespoon canola or safflower oil

1 white onion, thinly sliced

2 cloves garlic, finely chopped

½ teaspoon dried oregano, preferably Mexican

2 poblano chiles, roasted and seeded (page 106), then cut lengthwise into 12 strips each ¼ inch (6 mm) wide

½ teaspoon sea salt

½ lb (250 g) Muenster or Monterey jack cheese, shredded (about 2 cups)

12 fresh epazote leaves (optional)

Canola or safflower oil for deep-frying

Guacamole (page 10) for serving

Salsa Fresca (page 32) or Salsa Verde (page 111) for serving

To make the dough for the tortillas, in a bowl, mix the *masa harina* with the warm water. Using your hands, squish the flour and water together until a cohesive mass forms when pressed. The dough should be smooth and pliable. Cover the bowl with a barely damp kitchen towel and let stand for 5–10 minutes. Add the sea salt and knead gently in the bowl for 1 minute. Divide the dough into 12 equal portions and use your palms to form each portion into a ball. Cover with the damp towel. To make the filling, in a frying pan over medium heat, warm the oil. Add the onion and sauté until golden brown, about 5 minutes. Stir in the garlic and oregano and continue cooking for 1 minute. Add the chiles and sea salt and toss until everything is thoroughly heated. Taste and adjust the seasoning with sea salt.

To make the quesadillas, put 2 sheets of plastic cut from a plastic storage bag inside a tortilla press (page 115). Put a dough ball between the sheets and gently press down the top plate of the press. Remove the top piece of plastic and place a generous tablespoon of the shredded cheese on half of the tortilla, keeping the edges free. Top with 1 epazote leaf, if using, and a chile strip with a few onion slices. Lift the lower piece of plastic to fold the uncovered side of the tortilla over the filling. Press the edges together with your fingers, remove from the press, and set aside, covered with a barely damp towel. Repeat until all the quesadillas are made.

Preheat the oven to 200°F (95°C). Pour oil to a depth of 1 inch (2.5 cm) into a deep, heavy frying pan and place over medium-high heat until the oil shimmers. Fry the quesadillas, one at a time, until golden, 1–2 minutes. Using a slotted spatula, transfer to paper towels. Let drain briefly, then transfer to a heatproof platter and keep warm in the oven. Serve at once with the guacamole and salsa.

Note: Quick quesadillas may be made with thin, purchased white corn tortillas, but they will not seal as well as homemade tortillas.

MAKES 12 QUESADILLAS, OR 6 SERVINGS

MASA AND MASA HARINA

Masa, the dough used for making tortillas, tamales, and many *antojitos* (little bites) such as quesadillas, is the foundation of much of Mexican cooking. It is made by boiling dried corn kernels with slaked lime to remove their tough skins, and then grinding them to form the dough. If possible, use freshly ground *masa* from a local tortilla factory or other source—there is nothing like it. *Masa* can also be made from packaged *masa harina* (shown above), which is ground dried *masa,* but it will not have the same body or flavor as the freshly made dough.

SHRIMP EMPANADITAS

ABOUT EMPANADAS

Half-moon-shaped empanadas and *empanaditas,* their miniature look-alikes, are similar to the pielike pastries and turnovers of Spain and were baked in Mexico and Latin America as soon as the Spanish settlers began to grow wheat. The tender flour crusts may hold savory or sweet fillings. *Empanaditas* are ideal party fare because they can be made in advance and refrigerated overnight, or frozen for up to 2 months before baking. Bake frozen *empanaditas* in a preheated 350°F (180°C) oven until lightly browned, 20–30 minutes.

To make the filling, in a large frying pan over medium heat, warm the oil. Add the onion and garlic and sauté until soft but not browned, about 2 minutes. Add the tomatoes, bay leaves, and sea salt and pepper to taste, reduce the heat to medium-low, and continue to cook, stirring occasionally, until the mixture is dry, 10–15 minutes. Add the shrimp, chiles and pickling liquid, olives, and capers and stir until the shrimp are opaque and the mixture is dry, about 5 minutes. Remove from the heat, remove and discard the bay leaves, and set aside to cool for at least 30 minutes or, preferably, let cool completely, cover, and refrigerate overnight. Taste and adjust the seasoning with sea salt and pepper. The filling should be full flavored and highly seasoned.

To make the dough, in a bowl, using a large wooden spoon, beat together the butter and cream cheese until well blended. Stir in the flour and ½ teaspoon sea salt and mix well. Knead the dough just until it holds together and can be formed into a ball. Wrap with plastic wrap and refrigerate for 15 minutes.

Preheat the oven to 375°F (190°C). Lightly grease a baking sheet. On a lightly floured work surface, divide the dough in half. Roll out one half until it is ⅛ inch (3 mm) thick. Using a 3-inch (7.5-cm) biscuit or cookie cutter, cut out rounds. Place a heaping teaspoon of the filling in the center of each round, fold the round in half, and seal securely by pressing with your fingers. Use the tines of a fork to crimp the edges.

In a small bowl, beat the egg with ½ teaspoon water. Brush the tops of the half-moons with the egg mixture and place on the prepared baking sheet. Bake the *empanaditas* until lightly browned, about 15 minutes. Transfer to a wire rack and let cool for at least 5 minutes. Serve warm or at room temperature.

MAKES 30 EMPANADITAS

FOR THE FILLING:

2 tablespoons canola or safflower oil

½ white onion, finely chopped

3 cloves garlic, minced

1½ lb (750 g) ripe tomatoes, peeled and finely chopped

2 bay leaves

Sea salt and freshly ground pepper

1 lb (500 g) shrimp (prawns), peeled and chopped into ¼-inch (6-mm) pieces

4 pickled jalapeño or serrano chiles, finely chopped, with 1 tablespoon pickling liquid

8 pimiento-stuffed green olives, chopped

12 capers, finely chopped

FOR THE DOUGH:

1 cup (8 oz/250 g) unsalted butter, at room temperature

6 oz (185 g) low-fat cream cheese, at room temperature

2 cups (10 oz/315 g) unbleached all-purpose (plain) flour

Sea salt

1 large egg

FLAUTAS WITH SHREDDED CHICKEN

1 tablespoon canola or safflower oil, plus oil for frying

½ white onion, finely chopped (about ¾ cup/ 4 oz/125 g)

3 serrano or jalapeño chiles, finely chopped

2 cloves garlic, minced

1 large, ripe tomato, finely chopped, or ½ cup (3 oz/ 90 g) drained canned diced tomato

2½ cups (15 oz/470 g) finely shredded poached chicken (page 113)

Sea salt

12 thin corn tortillas, about 6 inches (15 cm) in diameter

4 cups (8 oz/250 g) finely shredded romaine (cos) lettuce

1 teaspoon fresh lime juice

FOR THE GARNISHES:

½ cup (4 fl oz/125 ml) Salsa Verde (page 111), plus extra for serving (optional)

½ cup (4 fl oz/125 ml) *crema* (page 51), plus extra for serving (optional)

6 radishes, trimmed and sliced

In a frying pan over medium-high heat, warm the 1 tablespoon oil. Add the onion, chiles, and garlic and sauté until softened, about 2 minutes. Stir in the tomato and continue to cook, stirring constantly, until the mixture thickens and the color changes, about 3 minutes. Fold in the chicken, season to taste with sea salt, and heat thoroughly. Remove from the heat and set aside.

Place a heavy frying pan or a stove-top griddle over medium-high heat until hot. Lay a tortilla briefly on the hot surface to make it pliable. Transfer it to a flat work surface and arrange several table-spoons of the chicken filling across the lower third of the tortilla. Tightly roll the tortilla up into a tube to make a *flauta*, secure with a toothpick, and set aside. Repeat with the remaining tortillas.

In a bowl, toss the lettuce with the lime juice. Spread it out on a serving plate or on individual plates, dividing it evenly.

Pour oil to a depth of at least ¾ inch (2 cm) into a deep, heavy frying pan and heat over medium-high heat until the oil shimmers and registers 350°F (180°C) on a deep-frying thermometer. Add the *flautas*, 2 or 3 at a time, and fry until crisp and pale gold on all sides, about 4 minutes. Using a slotted spoon or tongs, transfer them to paper towels to drain. Keep warm in a low oven while frying the rest.

Place all the *flautas* on the lettuce on the platter, or arrange 2 or 3 *flautas* on each plate. Spoon the ½ cup salsa across the *flautas* in a ribbon, then top with the ½ cup *crema* and the radishes. Serve at once, accompanied with more salsa and *crema*, if desired.

Make-Ahead Tip: The flautas *can be filled up to 45 minutes in advance of frying, if wrapped in plastic wrap and kept at room temperature.*

MAKES 4–6 SERVINGS

HANDLING FRESH CHILES

Chiles vary in pungency and in flavor. Capsaicin, the odorless, tasteless chemical responsible for the degree of "heat" in different chiles, is concentrated in the membranes that line the inside wall of the pod, with the seeds and the skin harboring a lesser dose by association. To reduce the fieriness of a chile, remove the seeds and membranes before using. Capsaicin, which is not water soluble, can cause pain if it comes into contact with eyes or other sensitive parts of the body. If possible, wear disposable gloves when handling chiles.

SQUID AND SHRIMP TOSTADAS

Clean the squid if needed *(left),* and cut the squid bodies crosswise into rings ½ inch (12 mm) wide. Keep the tentacles together unless large; if large, cut in half vertically. In a saucepan over medium heat, bring 2 cups (16 fl oz/500 ml) water to a boil. Add 1 teaspoon sea salt and the squid and cook until just opaque, about 1 minute. Quickly rinse under very cold running water until cold. Drain and pat dry with paper towels. In a bowl, stir together the squid and onion, then stir in the orange juice and the ½ cup lime juice. Add the chiles and pickling liquid and the carrots and toss lightly. Stir in the olive oil and season to taste with sea salt and pepper. Cover and refrigerate for at least 2 hours or for up to 1 day to allow the flavors to blend.

Spread the tortillas in a single layer, cover with a heavy kitchen towel to prevent curling, and let dry for several hours. About 1 hour before serving, remove the squid mixture from the refrigerator, stir in the shrimp, and taste and adjust the seasoning. Let stand at room temperature while frying the tortillas.

Preheat the oven to 200°F (95°C). To fry the tortillas, pour oil to a depth of 1 inch (2.5 cm) into a heavy, deep frying pan and heat to 375°F (190°C) on a deep-frying thermometer (see Note, page 10). Add the tortillas one at a time and fry until crisp, about 20 seconds. Using tongs and a slotted spatula, transfer to paper towels to drain, then place on a heatproof plate or tray in the oven. Repeat until all the tortillas are fried.

Just before serving, drain off all the liquid from the squid mixture. In a bowl, using a pestle or fork, mash the avocado flesh with the ⅛ teaspoon lime juice and a sprinkle of sea salt, forming a slightly lumpy paste. Coat each tostada with some of the avocado mixture. Add a thin layer of lettuce and top with the seafood mixture. Garnish with the cilantro leaves and eat out of hand.

MAKES 6 MAIN-COURSE OR 12 APPETIZER SERVINGS

1½ lb (750 g) small cleaned squid, or 2½ lb (1.25 kg) uncleaned squid

Sea salt and freshly ground pepper

½ small red onion, finely chopped

1 cup (8 fl oz/250 ml) fresh orange juice

½ cup (4 fl oz/125 ml) fresh lime juice, plus ⅛ teaspoon

3 pickled jalapeño chiles, sliced into thin rings, with 2 tablespoons pickling liquid

6 pickled carrots (packed in the jar with the pickled chiles), sliced into thin rings

½ cup (4 fl oz/125 ml) extra-virgin olive oil

12 corn tortillas, the thinnest possible, about 6 inches (15 cm) in diameter

6 oz (185 g) cooked small shrimp, chopped if desired

Canola or safflower oil for frying

1 ripe Hass avocado, pitted and peeled (page 10)

2 cups (4 oz/125 g) finely shredded iceberg lettuce

Leaves from 6 fresh cilantro (fresh coriander) sprigs

SOUPS AND SALADS

Soups are an integral part of most Mexican meals, and some may be served as a brothy or creamy first course. Many soups, however, are commonly served as one-pot meals, such as the pozole *in this chapter. Salads of lettuce and tomatoes are not a traditional part of Mexican cuisine; but, salads with regional ingredients, such as nopales and watercress, are not uncommon and can add refreshing flavors and textures to many Mexican meals.*

TORTILLA SOUP

In a blender or food processor, process the tomatoes, onion, and garlic until smooth, adding a small amount of the chicken stock if the mixture is too dry. In a Dutch oven or large *cazuela* or saucepan over medium-high heat, heat the oil until it is shimmering but not smoking. Pour in the tomato mixture all at once and fry, stirring frequently, until it thickens and darkens, about 4 minutes.

Add the stock and bring to a boil. Season to taste with sea salt, reduce the heat to medium-low, cover, and simmer for 5 minutes. Add the epazote and continue to simmer for another 5 minutes.

To prepare the condiments, heat the oil in a small frying pan over medium heat. Add the chiles and fry quickly until crisp, about 1 minute. Using a slotted spoon, transfer the chiles to paper towels to drain, then pat them with more paper towels to absorb the excess oil.

When ready to serve, remove the epazote sprigs from the soup. Put equal amounts of the tortilla strips and cheese in the bottom of each warmed bowl. Ladle in the hot soup and top with the fried chiles and the avocado. Serve at once.

Notes: To make the tortilla strips or squares, follow the instructions on page 10 for tortilla chips, using only 9 tortillas and cutting them into strips 1 inch (2.5 cm) long by ¼ inch (6 mm) wide or into ½-inch (12-mm) squares instead of wedges. Fry as directed and let cool before using. Queso Chihuahua *is a very flavorful Mexican cheese, but it may be difficult to find. A melting cheese such as Muenster is a good substitute for this recipe.*

MAKES 6 SERVINGS

EPAZOTE

Considered a tenacious weed by many gardeners, pungent epazote (also called wormseed) is looked on as a culinary treasure by Mexican cooks. The herb grows easily in almost all climates, so look for seeds in garden stores or catalogs and for seedlings in nurseries. Note that epazote will spread easily if the clusters of ripe seeds are not cut off. Ideally, epazote is used fresh, but dried epazote, stocked in Mexican markets, can be used in beans and soups. Enclose about 1 teaspoon in a tea ball for easy removal of the woody stems. If using fresh epazote, add it toward the end of cooking.

3 field-ripe tomatoes, or 1 can (14½ oz/455 g) diced tomatoes, drained

½ cup (2 oz/60 g) coarsely chopped white onion

2 cloves garlic, coarsely chopped

6 cups (48 fl oz/1.5 l) chicken stock (page 110) or prepared low-sodium broth

1 tablespoon canola or corn oil

Sea salt

4 large fresh epazote sprigs

FOR THE CONDIMENTS:

1 tablespoon canola or safflower oil

2 pasilla chiles, seeded (page 108) and cut into small squares or strips

Tortilla strips or squares (see Notes)

½ lb (250 g) *queso Chihuahua* (see Notes) or Muenster cheese, cut into ¼-inch (6-mm) cubes

1 ripe Hass avocado, pitted and peeled (page 10), then diced

POZOLE VERDE

½ lb (250 g) pork neck bones, ordered in advance from the butcher and rinsed

8 cups (64 fl oz/2 l) chicken stock (page 110)

1 lb (500 g) boneless pork shoulder

½ white onion, plus ¼ white onion, coarsely chopped

3 cloves garlic, halved

Sea salt

3 lb (1.5 kg) packaged partially cooked *pozole (far right)* or *nixtamal*

4 serrano chiles

1 lb (500 g) tomatillos, husked and rinsed (page 17)

2 romaine (cos) lettuce leaves, torn into large pieces

3 radish leaves

2 cups (10 oz/315 g) raw hulled green pumpkin seeds

2 tablespoons canola oil

2 fresh epazote sprigs or flat-leaf (Italian) parsley sprigs

Small bowls of finely shredded cabbage, finely chopped white onion, thinly sliced radishes, and dried oregano for serving

8 lime quarters for serving

Put the pork bones, stock, pork shoulder, ½ onion, garlic, and 1½ teaspoons sea salt in a large pot. Bring to a boil over high heat, skimming off any foam from the surface. Reduce the heat to medium-low, cover partially, and cook until the meat is tender, about 2 hours. After about 1 hour, add the *pozole,* stir well, and continue cooking. Meanwhile, bring a saucepan three-fourths full of water to a boil over high heat, add the chiles and tomatillos, reduce the heat to medium-low, and simmer until the tomatillos are soft, about 10 minutes. Drain through a sieve. Working in 2 batches, spoon half of the tomatillo mixture into a blender and add half each of the remaining chopped onion, the lettuce and radish leaves, and 1 cup (8 fl oz/250 ml) of the pork broth. Process until smooth. Pour into a bowl and repeat for the second batch. Set aside.

In a frying pan over medium heat, toast the pumpkin seeds, shaking the pan frequently, just until they swell and begin to tan, about 4 minutes. Remove from the heat, let cool, then grind in a spice grinder. In a large frying pan over medium-high heat, heat the oil. Add the ground seeds and fry, stirring frequently, until pastelike, about 2 minutes. Stir in the tomatillo purée, reduce the heat to medium-low, and continue to cook, stirring occasionally, until thick and rich, about 5 minutes. Remove from the heat.

Remove the pork and bones from the pot and let cool. Stir some of the remaining pork broth into the seed mixture. Pass the mixture through a medium-mesh sieve placed over the pot, pressing on the contents with the back of a spoon. Bring to a simmer over medium heat and cook for 30 minutes. Shred the pork and add it to the pot along with any meat from the bones. Discard the bones. Add the epazote and 2 teaspoons sea salt, stir well, and simmer for 20–30 minutes longer. Ladle the pozole into bowls and serve with the cabbage, finely chopped onion, radishes, oregano, and limes.

MAKES 8–10 SERVINGS

POZOLE

Corn, the very heart and soul of Mexican cooking, becomes something quite different when it is transformed into *pozole,* also known as hominy. Large, white corn kernels are treated with a softening solution of lime (calcium hydroxide), just as they are for making *masa* (page 35), but the kernels, rather than being ground, are cooked until tender. Look for packaged partially cooked *pozole (nixtamal)* at Mexican markets. You can substitute the *pozole* in this recipe with 4 cans (15 oz/470 g each) drained and rinsed white hominy. Add it to the soup along with the pumpkin seed mixture.

BLACK BEAN SOUP

BLACK BEANS

Beans are one of the most common foods of the Mexican people, and seldom a day goes by without a person eating them at least once. They come in a virtual kaleidoscope of earthy colors, especially in the central and northern parts of Mexico, but in the south, tiny black beans are simply cooked in a pot with onion and epazote or avocado leaves to add flavor. Always buy dried beans from a store with high turnover so that they are as fresh as possible and need the least amount of cooking time.

Pick over the beans and discard any broken beans or grit. Rinse the beans well, place in a large pot, and add 8 cups (64 fl oz/2 l) hot water. The water should cover the beans by at least 1 inch (2.5 cm). Add the onion, garlic, and lard and bring to a boil over high heat. Reduce the heat to medium, cover partially, and cook until tender, 2–4 hours. The timing will depend on the age of the beans. If using epazote rather than cilantro, add it now along with 2 teaspoons sea salt and continue to cook until the beans are soft, about 30 minutes longer. Add more hot water if needed to keep the level of the water at least 1 inch (2.5 cm) above the beans. Remove from the heat and let cool slightly.

Working in batches, transfer the beans to a blender, add the chiles, and process until velvety, adding a bit more liquid, if necessary, to thin to a medium consistency. Pour the purée back into the pot, and season to taste with sea salt. If using cilantro, add it now. Reheat over medium-low heat.

While the soup is heating, prepare the green onions. Cut off the root end of each green onion and leave about 2 inches (5 cm) of the green tops. In a frying pan over medium-high heat, warm the oil. Add the green onions and fry until browned on all sides, about 4 minutes. Remove from the heat and, when cool enough to handle, remove any tough outer layers of skin, slice into rounds, place in a bowl, and toss with a little sea salt.

Ladle the hot soup into warmed deep bowls. Top each serving with a swirl of *crema* and a sprinkling of the green onion slices.

Note: If your grill is fired up, you can brush the green onions with the oil and grill them over a hot fire (page 78).

Make-Ahead Tip: This soup can be made a day in advance and then reheated, adding more bean broth or water, if needed.

MAKES 6–8 SERVINGS

2 cups (14 oz/440 g) dried small black beans

½ white onion, quartered

4 large cloves garlic

1 tablespoon fresh pork lard (page 114), rendered bacon fat, or canola or safflower oil

3 large fresh epazote sprigs (optional) or fresh cilantro (fresh coriander) sprigs

Sea salt

2 canned *chiles chipotles en adobo,* coarsely chopped

8 plump green (spring) onions

2 tablespoons canola or safflower oil

1 cup (8 fl oz/250 ml) *crema* (page 51)

CREAMY POBLANO CHILE SOUP WITH CORN AND MUSHROOMS

1 tablespoon canola or safflower oil

1 white onion, coarsely chopped

2 cloves garlic

2 cups (12 oz/370 g) fresh or frozen corn kernels

3 poblano chiles, roasted, peeled, and seeded (page 106), then coarsely chopped

4 cups (32 fl oz/1 l) chicken stock (page 110) or prepared low-sodium broth

½ teaspoon dried oregano, preferably Mexican

2 tablespoons unsalted butter

½ lb (250 g) fresh chanterelle or other flavorful mushrooms such as cremini, brushed clean, trimmed, and sliced

Sea salt and freshly ground pepper

½ cup (4 fl oz/125 ml) *crema* (*far right*), thinned with milk

3 oz (90 g) Muenster cheese or farmers' cheese (see Note), cut into ¼-inch (6-mm) cubes, at room temperature

In a Dutch oven, *cazuela*, or other large pot over medium-low heat, heat the oil. Add the onion and sauté until golden and soft, about 2 minutes. Add the garlic and cook for 1 minute longer. Raise the heat to medium and add 1 cup (6 oz/185 g) of the corn, half of the chiles, and 1 cup (8 fl oz/250 ml) of the chicken stock. Bring to a simmer, stir in the oregano, and cook, uncovered, until the corn is tender, 10–15 minutes. Remove from the heat and let cool slightly.

Ladle the corn mixture into a blender with ½ cup (4 fl oz/125 ml) of the remaining chicken stock and process until smooth. Pass the mixture through a medium-mesh sieve back into the pot. Add the remaining stock and bring to a simmer over medium-low heat.

While the soup is heating, in a frying pan over medium heat, melt the butter. Add the remaining poblano chiles, the remaining corn, and the mushrooms and stir well. Season to taste with sea salt and pepper and sauté until the mushrooms release their liquid and then the liquid evaporates, about 8 minutes (this may take longer if you are using cremini).

Add the mushroom mixture and the *crema* to the soup, stir well, cover, and simmer for 10 minutes to blend the flavors. Taste and adjust the seasoning with sea salt and pepper.

Ladle the soup into warmed bowls and garnish with the cheese. Serve at once.

Note: Farmers' cheese is a white, crumbly, fresh form of cottage cheese from which most of the liquid has been removed. It is sold in a fairly solid loaf shape and is mild and slightly tangy. It is a nice alternative to Muenster cheese, which is more of a melting cheese, for this soup.

MAKES 6 SERVINGS

MEXICAN CREMA

Crema is a thick, slightly sour cream sold in Mexican markets. Crème fraîche, its French counterpart, is carried in some stores and can be substituted, or you can make your own *crema:* Mix 1 cup (8 fl oz/ 250 ml) heavy (double) cream (not ultrapasteurized) with 1 tablespoon buttermilk or plain yogurt with active cultures. Cover with plastic wrap, poke a few holes in the surface, and place in a warm spot (about 85°F/30°C) until thickened and set, 8–24 hours. Stir, cover, and refrigerate until chilled and firm before using or for up to 1 week.

WATERCRESS SALAD WITH ORANGE, JICAMA, AND AVOCADO

In a small bowl, whisk together the lime juice, chile, 1 teaspoon sea salt, and pepper to taste. Pour in the oil in a thin, steady stream while whisking constantly until thoroughly emulsified, forming a vinaigrette. Set aside.

Working with 1 orange at a time, cut a slice off the top and the bottom to reveal the flesh. Place the orange upright on the cutting board and, using a sharp knife, cut down along the sides, removing all the white pith and membrane. Cut the orange in half vertically then cut each half crosswise into slices ¼ inch (6 mm) thick. Repeat with the remaining orange. Place in a bowl, add the watercress and jicama, and toss to mix.

Just before serving, drizzle the vinaigrette over the watercress mixture, then carefully fold in the avocado slices. Taste and adjust the seasoning with sea salt. Serve at once.

MAKES 4 SERVINGS

JICAMA

A member of the large legume family, the crunchy, ivory-fleshed, brown-skinned jicama is a tuber used throughout Mexico, its country of origin. Jicama has a bland taste that benefits from being marinated raw in lime juice or from being combined with fruits or vegetables. Looking somewhat like drab turnips, jicamas can range in size from 5 oz (155 g) up to 5 lb (2.5 kg). At their best, they have a juicy, crisp flesh and a fairly thin skin. Before using, peel away the skin and the fibrous layer beneath it with a sharp knife.

⅓ cup (3 fl oz/80 ml) fresh lime juice, strained (about 2 limes)

1 serrano chile, thinly sliced

Sea salt and freshly ground pepper

½ cup (4 fl oz/125 ml) extra-virgin olive oil

2 navel oranges

2 bunches watercress, about ½ lb (250 g) total weight, large stems removed

1 small jicama, about ¾ lb (375 g), peeled *(far left)* and finely julienned

1 ripe Hass avocado, pitted and peeled (page 10), then sliced lengthwise

NOPALES SALAD

2 tablespoons canola oil

3 cloves garlic, finely chopped

1 lb (500 g) *nopales* (3 or 4), cleaned *(far right)* and cut into ¼-inch (6-mm) pieces

¼ cup (1½ oz/45 g) finely chopped white onion

2 jalapeño or serrano chiles, thinly sliced crosswise

Sea salt

FOR THE DRESSING:

1 teaspoon dried oregano, preferably Mexican

⅛ teaspoon Dijon mustard

2 tablespoons *each* cider vinegar and canola oil

Sea salt

Pinch of sugar

¾ lb (375 g) ripe tomatoes, diced

5 green (spring) onions, thinly sliced, including tender green parts

4–5 tablespoons (⅓ oz/10 g) finely minced fresh cilantro (fresh coriander)

6 inner leaves from 1 head romaine (cos) lettuce

¼ lb (125 g) *queso fresco* or mild feta cheese, crumbled

To cook the *nopales,* in a large, heavy frying pan or wide saucepan over medium heat, heat the oil. Add the garlic and fry for several seconds until fragrant. Stir in the *nopales,* onion, and chiles, cover, and cook, stirring occasionally, until the cactus is almost tender, about 15 minutes. The cactus will give off a sticky substance, but most of it will disappear with longer cooking. Uncover and continue to cook until the sticky residue has dried up, about 15 minutes longer. Season to taste with sea salt.

While the *nopales* are cooking, make the dressing. In a small bowl, whisk together the oregano, mustard, and vinegar. Whisk in the oil, ⅛ teaspoon sea salt, and the sugar.

Place the warm *nopales* in a bowl. Quickly whisk the dressing to recombine, then pour over the *nopales.* Toss to coat. Add the tomatoes and green onions and mix gently, coating all the vegetables with the dressing. Just before serving, add the cilantro and toss to mix.

Line each plate with a romaine leaf and top each leaf with a scoop of the *nopales* mixture. Scatter the cheese evenly over the salads. Serve at once.

Variation Tip: If fresh nopales *are unavailable, substitute 1 jar (30 oz/940 g)* nopales, *drained and rinsed. Add them after the garlic, onion, and chiles have cooked for 5 minutes.*

MAKES 6 SERVINGS

NOPALES

The paddles, or *nopales,* of the prickly pear (or nopal) cactus are sold in Mexican markets and many supermarkets, usually with their stickers already removed. They have a flavor that recalls both sorrel and asparagus and are used in salads, side dishes, and with eggs. *Nopales* are easy to prepare: Using a swivel-bladed vegetable peeler or a small paring knife, carefully cut away any stickers and their "eyes." Trim off the entire outer edge of the paddle, including the base end where it was attached to the cactus. A sticky fluid will exude, but will disappear when cooked, or it can be rinsed off.

SEAFOOD AND POULTRY

Over half the states in Mexico include shoreline, so it is no wonder that seafood plays a major part in the cuisine. Ducks and turkeys, which are native to Mexico, have also always been part of the diet. Chicken was introduced by the Spanish, and each region has its own specialty, whether served with a sauce, shredded and used as a filling, or baked in banana leaves. Here are recipes that reflect the wide range of ingredients and flavors in Mexican cooking.

SHRIMP IN CHIPOTLE SAUCE

PREPARING SHRIMP

To prepare a shrimp, pull or cut off the head with a knife. Tear off the legs on the inside curve of the body and pull off the shell, beginning at the head end and leaving the tail intact if specified in the recipe. The dark, veinlike intestinal tract that runs down the back of the shrimp is innocuous but is often removed for aesthetic reasons. To remove it, use a small, sharp knife to cut a small groove along the back of the shrimp. With the tip of the knife, lift out and gently scrape away the dark tract.

In a bowl, stir together the garlic, lime juice, and sea salt and pepper to taste. Add the shrimp and toss until thoroughly coated. Let marinate while preparing the sauce, at least 5 minutes.

In a heavy frying pan or *cazuela* over medium-high heat, heat the olive oil. Add the onion and sauté until golden, about 3 minutes. Add the tomatoes and cook, stirring constantly, just until the color deepens, less than 1 minute. Using a slotted spoon, transfer the tomato mixture to a blender, allowing any excess oil to drip back into the pan. Reserve the oil in the pan. Add the chiles and sauce, cola, and oregano to the blender. Process until you get a textured sauce.

Remove the shrimp from the marinade and pat dry with paper towels. Return the pan with the reserved oil to medium-high heat and heat until the oil begins to shimmer. Add half of the shrimp and cook until opaque, about 2 minutes. Using the slotted spoon, transfer to a plate. Repeat with the remaining shrimp and add them to the plate.

Return the still-hot pan to medium-high heat and add the sauce. Fry, stirring frequently, until the sauce thickens and the flavors deepen, about 5 minutes. Stir in the shrimp and cook for 2 minutes longer just to heat through. Divide the shrimp evenly among warmed individual plates. Spoon some of the remaining chipotle sauce over each serving and serve at once.

Note: Since the early 1940s, when colas were first introduced to Mexico, they have frequently been used to replace piloncillo *(page 93) in simple cooked dishes such as this one since they are frequently so easily available, adding flavor as well as sweetness.*

Serving Tip: Serve the shrimp over White Rice (page 110).

MAKES 4 OR 5 SERVINGS

8 cloves garlic, minced

¼ cup (2 fl oz/60 ml) fresh lime juice

Sea salt and freshly ground pepper

20 large shrimp (prawns), peeled and deveined, with tails intact *(far left)*

¼ cup (2 fl oz/60 ml) extra-virgin olive oil

½ cup (2½ oz/75 g) finely chopped white onion

4 ripe tomatoes, about 1½ lb (750 g), chopped, or 2 cans (14½ oz/455 g each) chopped tomatoes

2 canned *chiles chipotles en adobo* with 1 table-spoon sauce

½ cup (4 fl oz/125 ml) Coca-Cola or Pepsi-Cola (see Note)

¼ teaspoon dried oregano, preferably Mexican

SEA BASS IN PARCHMENT WITH SALSA VERDE

6 sea bass fillets or steaks, each 5–6 oz (155–185 g) and about ¾ inch (2 cm) thick

Sea salt

½ lb (250 g) tomatillos, husked and rinsed (page 17), then coarsely chopped

2 bunches fresh cilantro (fresh coriander), large stems removed, coarsely chopped

1 bunch fresh flat-leaf (Italian) parsley, large stems removed, coarsely chopped

3 fresh mint sprigs, coarsely chopped

3 jalapeño chiles, coarsely chopped

5 cloves garlic, coarsely chopped

¼ white onion, coarsely chopped

¾ cup (6 fl oz/180 ml) dry white wine or water

⅓ cup (3 fl oz/80 ml) extra-virgin olive oil

Preheat the oven to 450°F (230°C). Remove the skin from the fish if it is still intact and run your fingers over the fish to check for and remove any embedded bones, using tweezers if necessary. Sprinkle with sea salt on both sides.

In a blender, process the tomatillos, cilantro, parsley, mint, chiles, garlic, onion, and wine until very smooth and thick; a few tomatillo seeds will dot the sauce. Season to taste with sea salt.

Cut 6 sheets of parchment (baking) paper large enough to easily contain one piece of fish. Fold each piece in half lengthwise. Unfold and brush the center of each sheet with some of the olive oil. Spoon 3 tablespoons of the sauce in the center of one half of each sheet of parchment, place a fillet on top of the sauce, and rub the fish generously with oil. Cover with another ½ cup (4 fl oz/ 125 ml) of the sauce, making certain it does not come close to the edge. Fold the uncovered half of the parchment over the fish and cut the paper around each portion with scissors, beginning at the fold and forming a half heart all around the fish and leaving a distance of 1½ inches (4 cm) around the edge. Seal the packets by pleating the edges (right). Place the packets on a baking sheet.

Bake the packets for 10 minutes. If the packets are tightly sealed, they will balloon up and fill with hot steam.

Remove the packets from the oven and place on warmed plates. Carefully open the packets with scissors and serve at once.

Note: You may also prepare this recipe using aluminum foil instead of parchment paper.

Serving Tip: Accompany with White Rice (page 110).

MAKES 6 SERVINGS

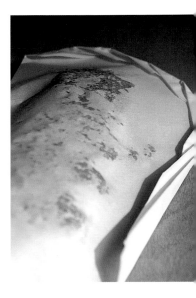

COOKING IN PARCHMENT

Tightly sealing fish in a wrapping of herbaceous leaves, which allows the fish to steam gently in its own juices, is a traditional technique in Mexican cooking. This recipe uses parchment paper instead, which lacks the flavors imparted by the leaves, but the method captures the juices and makes a dramatic presentation when the package is opened. (Take care when opening; the trapped steam can cause burns.) To seal the parchment, starting at an open corner, fold over the open edge, overlapping the fold on itself at 1-inch (2.5-cm) intervals to form flat pleats.

RICE WITH SEAFOOD

Peel and devein the shrimp, reserving the shells and leaving the tails intact (page 58). Remove the skin from the fish if it is still intact and run your fingers over the fillet to check for and remove any embedded bones, using tweezers if necessary. Cut the fish into 1-inch (2.5-cm) pieces. Sprinkle the shrimp and fish generously with sea salt and pepper and refrigerate until needed.

Put the shrimp shells and fish stock in a saucepan and season to taste with sea salt. Bring to a boil over high heat, reduce the heat to medium, cover, and simmer for 20 minutes. Remove from the heat and strain into a measuring pitcher. Add enough water to bring the liquid to 4 cups (32 fl oz/1 l).

In a Dutch oven over medium heat, heat the oil. Add the onion and garlic and sauté until softened, about 2 minutes. Stir in the rice and cook until golden, about 3 minutes. Add the tomatoes and cook, stirring often, to combine the flavors, 4–5 minutes. Pour in 2 cups (16 fl oz/500 ml) of the reserved stock and bring to a boil. As soon as the liquid boils, reduce the heat to medium-low, cover, and cook for about 5 minutes. Uncover, stir in the chiles and chives, and add the remaining 2 cups stock. Re-cover and continue cooking for 5 minutes longer.

Uncover and stir in the fish, shrimp, and clams, discarding any clams that do not close to the touch. Reduce the heat to low, re-cover, and cook, stirring occasionally if necessary to prevent sticking, until the rice is tender, 8–10 minutes. Discard any clams that failed to open. Add 1 teaspoon sea salt and ½ teaspoon pepper, then taste and adjust the seasoning. Stir in the chopped cilantro. The mixture should be the consistency of thick soup with some liquid remaining. Spoon the rice and seafood into warmed individual large, shallow bowls or into a warmed shallow serving bowl. Garnish with the cilantro sprigs and serve at once.

MAKES 4–6 SERVINGS

RICE

The Spanish brought rice with them to Mexico, and it has become an indispensable part of Mexican cooking ever since. Mexican cooks adopted the Spanish pilaf method of briefly frying the kernels with onion and garlic in oil before adding the liquid. But they did not adopt the stubby Valencia rice of Spain, preferring instead longer, more slender grains. For this dish, known as *arroz a la tumbada* and reminiscent of paella, a medium-grain rice imported from Valencia works best, as it will absorb the liquid better than other varieties. An American-grown medium-grain rice will also work well.

1 lb (500 g) large shrimp (prawns) in the shell (20–30 shrimp)

¾ lb (375 g) red snapper or sea bass fillet

Sea salt and freshly ground pepper

4 cups (32 fl oz/1 l) fish stock or bottled clam juice

½ cup (4 fl oz/125 ml) canola or corn oil

½ white onion, halved vertically and thinly sliced crosswise

5 cloves garlic, finely chopped

1½ cups (10½ oz/330 g) medium-grain white rice, rinsed and drained

3 large, ripe plum (Roma) tomatoes, finely chopped

3 jalapeño chiles, roasted and seeded (page 106), then cut lengthwise into strips

3 tablespoons minced fresh chives

12 clams, well scrubbed

4–6 tablespoons (⅓–½ oz/ 10–15 g) chopped fresh cilantro (fresh coriander) leaves, plus 6 sprigs

ZUCCHINI-STUFFED CHICKEN BREASTS

5 tablespoons (2½ fl oz/ 75 ml) canola or safflower oil

¼ cup (1 oz/30 g) finely diced white onion

1 clove garlic, finely minced

¾ cup (3 oz/90 g) finely chopped zucchini (about 1 small)

4 skinless, boneless chicken breast halves

Sea salt and freshly ground pepper

3 poblano chiles, roasted and seeded (page 106)

4 slices Monterey jack cheese, each 2 inches (5 cm) long, 1 inch (2.5 cm) wide, and ⅛ inch (3 mm) thick

FOR THE SAUCE:

Reserved chopped poblano chiles

¼ white onion, roasted *(far right)*

1 clove garlic, roasted *(far right)*

1 cup (8 fl oz/250 ml) half-and-half (half cream)

2 tablespoons unsalted butter

Sea salt

In a heavy frying pan over medium heat, heat 2 tablespoons of the oil. Add the onion and sauté until just starting to turn pale yellow, about 2 minutes. Stir in the garlic and sauté for several seconds, then add the zucchini and cook until softened, 1–2 minutes longer. Remove from the heat, drain off any oil, and let cool. Trim off any excess fat from the chicken breasts. One at a time, place the breasts between 2 sheets of plastic wrap or waxed paper and, using a rolling pin or the flat side of a meat mallet, pound them gently, working from the center outward, until an even ⅛ inch (3 mm) thick. Sprinkle the chicken breasts on both sides with ¼ teaspoon sea salt. Coarsely chop 2½ of the chiles and reserve to use for the sauce. Cut the remaining ½ chile lengthwise into 4 strips.

Lay out the chicken breasts, smooth side down, and spread a fourth of the zucchini mixture evenly over each breast, leaving a ½-inch (12-mm) border on all sides. Lay 1 chile strip and 1 cheese strip across the narrow side of the chicken. Starting at a narrow end, carefully roll up each breast, making at least 1 full turn and forming a tight, fat tube. Secure with toothpicks. In a large, heavy frying pan over medium-high heat, heat the remaining 3 table-spoons oil. Add the rolls and lightly brown on all sides, turning as each side starts to color, about 6 minutes. Sprinkle with sea salt and pepper. Reduce the heat to medium and continue cooking, turning frequently, until the meat is opaque throughout, 10–15 minutes.

Meanwhile, make the sauce. In a blender, process the reserved chiles, the onion, garlic, and half-and-half until smooth. In a small saucepan, melt the butter over low heat. Pour in the sauce and stir constantly until the mixture thickens, about 5 minutes. Season to taste with sea salt. Keep warm over low heat. To serve, slice each roll crosswise into 3 or 4 rounds. Divide among warmed individual plates, spoon the chile sauce over the top, and serve.

MAKES 4 SERVINGS

ROASTING ONIONS AND GARLIC

Roasting onions and garlic will intensify their flavor. To roast onions, cut as directed in the recipe. Prepare a medium-hot fire in a charcoal or gas grill, or line a griddle or heavy frying pan with aluminum foil, shiny side up, and place over medium heat. Add the onion and cook, turning often, until blackened in spots and starting to soften, about 10 minutes. Let cool and remove and discard any outer papery skin. Roast garlic in the same way, separating, but not peeling, each clove and removing any loose papery skin. Roast until the skins blacken. Let cool before peeling.

PIBIL-STYLE BAKED CHICKEN

PIBIL COOKING

On the Yucatán peninsula, chicken, turkey, and pork are traditionally marinated and slowly cooked over coals in a pit, or *pib,* in a method known as *pibil* cooking. Elsewhere, a conventional oven can be used. What cannot be substituted, however, is the marinade made from *achiote* paste, which gives this dish its characteristic earthy flavor. Equally important is enclosing the food in fragrant banana leaves. Look for the leaves frozen or occasionally fresh, in Mexican and Asian groceries.

Rinse the chicken pieces and pat dry with paper towels. Prick the chicken skin in several places with the tip of a sharp knife so that the marinade will penetrate. In a small bowl, stir together the bitter orange juice, diluted *achiote* paste, garlic, and 1 teaspoon sea salt. Rub the chicken pieces all over with the mixture, then slip them into a zippered plastic bag, seal closed, and refrigerate for at least 2 hours or up to overnight.

Preheat the oven to 375°F (190°C). Lay out 8 of the banana-leaf pieces, shiny side up. Tear the remaining leaf into 8 strips, ½ inch (12 mm) wide, to use as ties (they may need to be knotted together). Remove the chicken from the plastic bag, reserving the marinade. Layer half of the fresh onion and tomato slices in the centers of 4 of the leaves. Top with a piece of the marinated chicken and a few strips of the chile. Top with the remaining fresh onion and tomato slices. Drizzle on some of the marinade. Cover with another leaf, shiny side down, folding the edges together to seal. Tie each packet of chicken together with the ties.

Cut out 4 pieces of aluminum foil, each about 12 by 14 inches (30 by 35 cm). Wrap each banana-leaf packet in a piece of aluminum foil and tightly crimp the edges until completely sealed. Place the packets on a baking sheet.

Bake the packets for 30 minutes. Turn the packets over and cook for another 20 minutes. Remove 1 packet from the oven, open it, and using a knife, cut into the thickest part of the chicken; it should be opaque throughout. If it is not, rewrap and return to the oven for a few more minutes.

To serve, remove the aluminum foil and place each banana-leaf packet on an individual plate. Open the packets, top each portion with one-fourth of the marinated onion slices, and serve at once.

MAKES 4 SERVINGS

1 large chicken, about 4 lb (2 kg), skin intact and cut into 4 pieces (2 leg-and-thigh pieces and 2 breast halves)

2 tablespoons fresh bitter orange juice (page 113)

2 teaspoons *achiote* paste (page 113), diluted with 2 teaspoons water

2 cloves garlic, finely chopped

Sea salt

9 pieces banana leaves, each approximately 16 inches (40 cm) square, defrosted if frozen

1 red onion, thinly sliced

2 tomatoes, thickly sliced

1 small güero chile, seeded (page 39) and cut lengthwise into narrow strips

1 cup (3½ oz/105 g) Marinated Red Onion slices (page 115)

TINGA POBLANA WITH CHICKEN

4 chicken thighs, about 1 lb (500 g) total weight

½ white onion, cut into chunks, plus 1 cup (5 oz/ 155 g) finely chopped

4 cloves garlic, 2 cloves slightly smashed and 2 cloves finely chopped

Sea salt

1 tablespoon canola or safflower oil

½ lb (250 g) Mexican chorizo, casings removed and sausage crumbled

1 can (14½ oz/455 g) chopped tomatoes, drained

1 teaspoon dried oregano, preferably Mexican

2 bay leaves

2 canned *chiles chipotles en adobo* with 1 tablespoon sauce

FOR THE GARNISHES:

½ white onion, quartered vertically, thinly sliced cross- wise, and separated into quarter rings

2 ripe Hass avocados, pitted and peeled (page 10), then cut into ½-inch (12-mm) chunks

Place the chicken thighs, onion chunks, and smashed garlic in a saucepan and add water to cover. Add 1 teaspoon sea salt and bring to a boil over high heat, skimming off any foam that forms on the surface. Reduce the heat to medium-low and simmer, uncovered, until the chicken is opaque throughout, 20–30 minutes. Using tongs or a slotted spoon, transfer the chicken to a plate. Reserve the broth. When the chicken is cool enough to handle, remove and discard the skin and bones and coarsely shred the meat with your fingers.

In a large frying pan, Dutch oven, or *cazuela* over medium heat, heat the oil. Add the chorizo and fry for about 5 minutes. Discard the excess rendered fat from the pan, leaving just 1 tablespoon. Add the finely chopped onion and garlic and sauté until beginning to soften, but not yet starting to brown, about 1 minute. Add the shredded chicken, tomatoes, oregano, bay leaves, chiles and sauce, and about 1 cup (8 fl oz/250 ml) of the reserved broth to keep the mixture moist. Simmer, uncovered, until the flavors are blended, about 15 minutes. Add more broth to the pan if the mixture begins to stick, but do not add too much; the mixture should absorb the liquid and not be runny. Remove and discard the bay leaves and season to taste with sea salt. Scoop the chicken into a warmed serving dish and garnish with the onion and avocado.

Note: Tinga, a specialty of Puebla, means "disorder" in Spanish and refers to a dish of savory shredded meat often used as a filling for tacos.

Make-Ahead Tip: The chicken can be cooked up to 1 day in advance. Cover and refrigerate until needed. You can also prepare the entire dish 1–2 days in advance and then reheat it over low heat.

Serving Tips: Serve with warmed corn tortillas (page 115) for diners to use for making tacos, or spoon over White Rice (page 110).

MAKES 6 SERVINGS

CHORIZO

Mexican chorizo is ground pork heavily seasoned with chile and garlic, stuffed into casings, and hung for several days to allow the flavors to mellow before using. Unlike the milder, smoked Spanish chorizo, this sausage is never eaten without cooking. It can be purchased freshly made at Mexican markets and at many butcher shops. Never purchase chorizo prepackaged in plastic. Your dish will be greasy and of disappointing flavor. Spanish chorizo may be substituted, but add additional ground chile to the sausage once it is removed from its casings, or use hot Italian sausage.

DUCK IN A GREEN PIPIÁN

PIPIÁN

A thick sauce similar to a mole, a *pipián* always includes seeds, traditionally pumpkin, and often sesame seeds. To prepare the seeds for the *pipián* in this recipe, in a large, dry frying pan, toast the sesame seeds over medium heat until they start to turn golden, about 2 minutes. Let cool and transfer to a blender. In the same pan over medium heat, heat the oil.

Add the pumpkin seeds and toast, stirring constantly, until plump, 1–2 minutes; do not let brown. Using a slotted spoon, remove the seeds, reserving 2 tablespoons for garnish and adding the rest to the blender. Set aside the pan with the oil.

To make the stock, put all the giblets but the livers, the necks and backs, the onion, garlic, peppercorns, bay leaves, and 1 teaspoon sea salt in a large pot. Add cold water to cover and bring to a low boil over medium-high heat, skimming off any foam. Reduce the heat to low, partially cover, and simmer for at least 1½ hours or up to 4 hours. Remove from the heat. Pour through a sieve into a clean container. Let cool, cover, and refrigerate overnight. Lift off the solidified fat on the surface. You should have 7 cups (56 fl oz/1.75 l).

Trim off any excess fat from the duck pieces and season them with sea salt and pepper. Prick the skin with a sharp knife, being careful not to pierce the flesh. In a large, heavy frying pan over medium-high heat, heat the oil. Add the leg-and-thigh pieces, skin side down, and fry without turning, stopping to drain off the rendered fat from time to time, until browned, 10–15 minutes. Transfer to a plate and repeat to brown the breasts. Return the duck pieces to the pan, reduce the heat to medium-low, cover tightly, and cook until the meat is tender, about 40 minutes.

Prepare the seeds for the *pipián (left)*. In a saucepan over medium heat, cover the tomatillos with water. Bring to a simmer and cook until soft, about 10 minutes. Drain and add to the blender. Add the onion, chiles, garlic, epazote, and 1½ cups (12 fl oz/375 ml) of the duck stock and process until smooth, adding more stock if necessary. Pour through a medium-mesh sieve placed over a bowl.

Return the reserved frying pan with the oil to low heat and reheat the oil. Pour in the sauce and stir frequently for about 5 minutes. Gradually add 4½ cups (36 fl oz/1.1 l) stock and continue cooking over very low heat until the sauce thickly covers the back of a wooden spoon, about 10 minutes. Season to taste with sea salt. Add the duck pieces and warm thoroughly in the sauce. Transfer the duck to individual plates. Ladle the sauce over the duck, garnish with the reserved pumpkin seeds, and serve with the rice alongside.

MAKES 6–8 SERVINGS

2 ducks, 5–6 lb (2.5–3 kg) each, skin intact, cut into 4 pieces (2 leg-and-thigh pieces and 2 breast halves), giblets, neck, and back reserved for making stock

½ white onion, thickly sliced

2 cloves garlic

8 peppercorns

2 bay leaves

Sea salt and freshly ground pepper

1 tablespoon canola oil

FOR THE PIPIÁN:

½ cup (1½ oz/45 g) sesame seeds

2 tablespoons canola oil

1 cup (5 oz/155 g) raw hulled green pumpkin seeds, plus 2 tablespoons

12 tomatillos, husked and rinsed (page 17)

½ white onion, coarsely chopped

12 serrano chiles, coarsely chopped

8 cloves garlic, coarsely chopped

8 fresh epazote sprigs

Sea salt

White Rice (page 110) for serving

PORK, BEEF, AND LAMB

The self-sufficient and prolific pig is the major meat source in Mexico, and each region has its local specialty, with carnitas reigning supreme in Michoacán. A tender grilled beef steak is the featured ingredient in Mexico's original "combination plate" and also shredded in the cold meat salpicón *of the Yucatán. Lamb is also a favorite meat, and here you will find a recipe for lamb long simmered in mouth-tingling chile sauce.*

CARNITAS

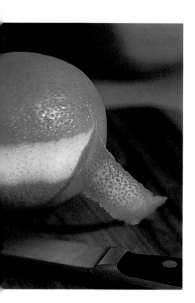

Cut off any big pieces of fat from the pork and put them into a wide, heavy saucepan or frying pan. Cut the pork into strips about 1½ inches (4 cm) long and ¾ inch (2 cm) wide. Add the pork to the pan with the garlic, orange zest, orange juice, and 2 teaspoons sea salt. The meat should be in a single layer, if possible. Add water to barely cover the meat and bring to a boil over medium heat. Reduce the heat to medium low, cover partially, and cook, stirring occasionally, until all of the liquid has evaporated, about 1 hour. If the meat is not yet fork tender, add a bit more water and continue cooking.

Uncover the pan and continue cooking the pork until all the fat is rendered and the meat is browning in the melted fat, 10–15 minutes longer. There is usually enough melted fat in the pan, but if necessary, add the 1 tablespoon oil. When the meat is brown and crisp, using a slotted spoon, transfer it to a colander and let any excess fat drain away.

Immediately transfer the pork to a warmed serving bowl. Accompany with the warm tortillas to make tacos: slather each tortilla with the guacamole and the salsa. Serve with the refried beans and/or the rice on the side.

MAKES 6 SERVINGS

ZESTING CITRUS

Most citrus fruits, except some that are grown organically, are coated with a thin layer of wax that must be scrubbed off before removing the zest, the colored portion of the peel. Although there are specialized utensils, called zesters, that can be used to take off narrow strips of this outer layer, a sharp paring knife or vegetable peeler also works well. Just be sure to remove as little of the bitter white pith beneath the zest as possible. For recipes calling for grated zest, use a Microplane grater or the finest rasps of a handheld grater. When buying oranges, don't worry if they are greenish; they will still be ripe.

3 lb (1.5 kg) boneless pork shoulder or country-style ribs

6 cloves garlic, halved

Zest of 1 orange, cut into strips *(far left)*

¾ cup (6 fl oz/180 ml) fresh orange juice

Sea salt

1 tablespoon canola or safflower oil, if needed

12 purchased corn or flour tortillas, 6–8 inches (15–20 cm) in diameter, warmed (page 115)

Guacamole (page 10) for serving

Salsa Fresca (page 32) for serving

Refried Beans (page 111) and/or Red Rice (page 110) for serving

PORK CHOPS MARINATED IN ADOBO SAUCE

FOR THE ADOBO SAUCE:

2 tablespoons canola or safflower oil

4 large ancho chiles, seeded (page 108) and torn into large pieces

4 cloves garlic, minced

Sea salt and freshly ground pepper

1 teaspoon sugar

1 teaspoon dried oregano, preferably Mexican

¼ teaspoon ground cumin, preferably freshly ground

⅛ teaspoon dried thyme

½ cup (4 fl oz/125 ml) cider vinegar

6 pork chops, between ¾–1 inch (2–2.5 cm) thick

1 tablespoon canola or safflower oil

½ cup (2 oz/60 g) thinly sliced white onion

8 radishes, trimmed and thinly sliced

To make the adobo sauce, in a frying pan over medium heat, heat the oil. When quite hot, add several pieces of the chile and press down on them until they begin to blister, a few seconds. Transfer the pieces to a bowl and repeat with the remaining chile pieces. Add hot water to cover, weight them down with a plate, and let soak for 15 minutes. Using a slotted spoon, transfer the chiles to a blender; reserve the chile water. Add the garlic, 1 tablespoon sea salt, ½ teaspoon pepper, the sugar, oregano, cumin, thyme, vinegar, and ½ cup (4 fl oz/125 ml) of the chile water to the blender and process until very smooth.

Spread both sides of each pork chop with the adobo sauce, cover, and refrigerate for at least 1 hour or preferably overnight.

In a large frying pan over medium-high heat, heat the oil. Add the chops and sear for just 1 minute on each side. Immediately reduce the heat to medium or medium-low; the chops should continue to sizzle in the oil. Cover and cook, turning once, until the chops are firm to the touch or an instant-read thermometer inserted into the thickest part of a chop away from the bone registers 145°F (63°C), 3–4 minutes on each side. Remove from the heat, cover loosely with aluminum foil, and let rest for 5 minutes. At this point the thermometer should read 150°F (65°C). Do not overcook or the meat will be dry.

Transfer the chops to warmed individual plates and top with the onion and radishes. Serve at once.

Make-Ahead Tip: The adobo sauce can be made any time in advance and refrigerated; it keeps indefinitely.

Serving Tip: Serve with small new potatoes that have been boiled until tender, brushed with a little of the adobo sauce, and quickly fried in a small amount of oil.

MAKES 6 SERVINGS

ADOBO SAUCE

In Mexico, adobo is a seasoning made from dried chiles, herbs, salt, and spices, ground together with vinegar to the consistency of a thick paste. It is similar to the Spanish mixture of same name, which calls for vinegar, olive oil, and spices. Because vinegar and salt are natural preservatives, the use of adobo was a traditional technique for pickling, and thus preserving, meats in both Spain and Mexico in the days before widespread refrigeration.

CARNE ASADA

Place a *comal,* griddle, or cast-iron frying pan over medium heat and heat until hot. Put the garlic cloves on the hot surface and toast until blackened and soft, about 8 minutes. Remove from the heat, let cool to the touch, and peel.

In a small bowl, using a fork, smash together the garlic and the chiles and sauce. Stir in the lime juice, oregano, and 1 teaspoon sea salt.

Coat the steaks on both sides with the chile mixture. Set aside at room temperature for 30–45 minutes, turning at least once.

Build a fire, preferably using mesquite charcoal, in an outdoor charcoal grill and let burn until covered with white ash. Leave the coals heaped in the center of the grill; do not spread them out. Brush the grill rack with oil.

Place the steaks on the grill rack directly over the coals and grill, turning at least once, until crusty brown on both sides and rare or medium-rare on the inside, 5–7 minutes total. Transfer to a warmed serving platter, cover loosely with aluminum foil, and let rest briefly before serving. Serve the steaks on large individual plates and accompany with the grilled onions and lots of *salsa fresca* and guacamole. Serve the pot beans in bowls alongside.

Serving Tip: Red Rice (page 110) and flour tortillas would be part of a grilled meal such as this in the cattle country of Mexico's northern border states, along with beans, guacamole, and salsa. Often, small tamales are also offered. In Guadalajara, a city in the western part of central Mexico, the steak might also be served with quesadillas and nopales salad (page 55).

MAKES 6 SERVINGS

GRILLED SPRING ONIONS

Small, fat spring onions, with bulbs about 1 inch (2.5 cm) in diameter, are usually available in farmers' markets in early summer. Fat green onions, or scallions, can be substituted. To prepare, slice off the root ends of about 4 onions per serving and trim away 1–2 inches (2.5–5 cm) of the tops. Rub the onions lightly with canola oil. Place a double layer of heavy-duty aluminum foil on the grill directly over high heat. Spread the onions out on the foil, with the white parts exposed over the coals. Grill, turning frequently, until browned on all sides, about 10 minutes. Toss with fresh lime juice before serving.

8 unpeeled cloves garlic

3 canned *chiles chipotles en adobo* with 1 teaspoon sauce

¼ cup (2 fl oz/60 ml) fresh lime juice, strained (about 2 limes)

2 tablespoons dried oregano, preferably Mexican

Sea salt

2 lb (1 kg) trimmed rib-eye or other steaks of choice, about ¾ inch (2 cm) thick

Canola or safflower oil for brushing grill rack

Grilled Spring Onions *(far left)* for serving

Salsa Fresca (page 32) for serving

Guacamole (page 10) for serving

Pot Beans (page 111), made with pinto beans, for serving

SALPICÓN OF BEEF

2 lb (1 kg) beef flank steak, cut into 2 equal pieces

1 white onion, thickly sliced, plus ½ white onion, thinly sliced, and ½ cup (2½ oz/ 75 g) finely chopped white onion

3 cloves garlic

6 peppercorns

2 bay leaves

1 tablespoon dried oregano, preferably Mexican

Sea salt and freshly ground pepper

½ cup (4 fl oz/125 ml) olive oil

¼ cup (2 fl oz/60 ml) fresh lime juice

4 pickled jalapeño or serrano chiles, finely chopped, with 2 tablespoons pickling liquid

½ cup (2 oz/60 g) cubed Monterey jack cheese (½-inch/12-mm cubes)

½ cup (½ oz/15 g) fresh cilantro (fresh coriander) leaves, chopped

Inner leaves from 1 small head romaine (cos) lettuce, plus 1 cup (2 oz/60 g) shredded romaine

1 firm but ripe Hass avocado, pitted, peeled, and sliced

Put the flank steak, thickly sliced onion, garlic, peppercorns, and bay leaves in a large pot or saucepan and add water to cover. Bring to a boil over high heat, then reduce the heat so that only a few bubbles occasionally rise to the surface. Skim off any foam that forms on the surface and add the oregano and 2 teaspoons sea salt. Let simmer until a piece of the flank steak shreds easily, 30–45 minutes.

While the beef cooks, in a frying pan over medium heat, heat the olive oil. Add the thinly sliced onion and sauté until translucent, about 4 minutes. Stir in the lime juice and chiles and pickling liquid and simmer until the flavors are well mingled, about 2 minutes. Remove from the heat and set aside.

When the beef is tender, remove the pan from the heat. Let the beef cool in the broth, then remove it from the broth. Measure out ½ cup (4 fl oz/125 ml) of the broth and reserve. Save the remaining broth for another use.

Trim off any excess fat from the beef, then finely shred the beef. Put it into a bowl with the ½ cup broth and let stand until all of the liquid has been absorbed by the beef, about 5 minutes. Add the onion mixture, cheese, and cilantro. Season to taste with sea salt and pepper, and then toss together with your hands or a fork until well mixed. Let rest for 15–20 minutes to allow the flavors to blend.

Make a bed of the whole romaine leaves on a platter. Mound the beef mixture on the lettuce and garnish with the avocado slices, shredded lettuce, and finely chopped onion. Serve at room temperature.

Serving Tip: This is an ideal buffet dish. Serve with warmed corn tortillas (page 115) and guacamole (page 10).

MAKES 6 SERVINGS

SALPICÓN

The Spanish word *salpicón* can be roughly translated as "jumble" or "hodgepodge," but this dish of shredded beef is anything but a haphazard mixture. It is always highly seasoned with chiles and embellished with onions and avocados, and sometimes with cheese. The flavorful mixture was originally made with the meat of a small native deer once prevalent on the Yucatán peninsula, but the Spanish, who enjoyed cold meat dishes, instead served it as a main-dish salad of beef. In its contemporary form, *salpicón* is occasionally made with everything from chicken to crab.

MEATBALLS IN CHIPOTLE SAUCE

To make the sauce, in a blender, combine the tomatoes, chiles and sauce, garlic, cumin, oregano, and ½ teaspoon sea salt. Add the beef stock and process until smooth. Taste and adjust with more sea salt, if needed, and blend again.

In a Dutch oven or *cazuela* over medium-high heat, heat 1 tablespoon of oil until it is shimmering but not smoking. Pour in the sauce and cook, stirring occasionally, until the sauce starts to thicken, about 3 minutes. Reduce the heat to medium-low and cook, uncovered, until the sauce has reduced and is a deep red, about 5 minutes. There should be just a few bubbles bursting on the surface.

While the sauce is cooking, make the meatballs. In a bowl, place the beef, pork, cumin, garlic, 1 teaspoon sea salt, and ¼ teaspoon pepper. Mix well with a fork or your hands. Stir in the bread crumbs, eggs, and milk, mixing thoroughly. In a small frying pan over medium-high heat, heat a little oil and fry a nugget of the meat mixture. Taste and adjust the seasoning of the mixture, if needed.

Form the meat mixture into 1½-inch (4-cm) balls, dropping each meatball into the sauce as it is made. Cover, reduce the heat to low, and simmer, stirring occasionally to make sure that all the meatballs cook evenly (the sauce will barely cover them all), until the meatballs are cooked through, about 20 minutes. If the meatballs start to stick, add some hot water. Serve directly from the pot or transfer to a warmed serving bowl and serve at once.

Note: To make the fresh bread crumbs, use any bread a few days past its peak of freshness. Cut off the crusts, tear into bite-sized pieces, and process in a blender or food processor until coarsely ground.

Serving Tip: Accompany with boiled or steamed tiny new potatoes or White Rice (page 110).

MAKES 6 SERVINGS

CHIPOTLE CHILES

The gutsy chipotle chile is very special, as it is one of the few chiles that is smoked after it is dried, giving it an unusual flavor and aroma. This dried ripened jalapeño chile is typically a leathery tan, with some varieties a deep burgundy, and it is used to flavor sauces, soups, and stews. The whole chiles are often stuffed. Outside of Mexico, chipotle chiles turn up most commonly as *chiles chipotles en adobo,* canned in a vinegar-tomato sauce. The chiles and their sauce are usually blended with other ingredients, such as tomatoes, before adding to various savory dishes to give them a hot, smoky flavor.

FOR THE SAUCE:

4 ripe tomatoes, roasted (page 108), or 1 can (14½ oz/455 g) diced tomatoes, with juice

2 canned *chiles chipotles en adobo* with 1 teaspoon sauce

2 cloves garlic

¼ teaspoon ground cumin

½ teaspoon dried oregano, preferably Mexican

Sea salt

1 cup (8 fl oz/250 ml) beef stock (page 110) or prepared low-sodium broth

Canola or safflower oil

FOR THE MEATBALLS:

¾ lb (375 g) ground (minced) beef

¾ lb (375 g) lean ground (minced) pork

½ teaspoon ground cumin

1 clove garlic, minced

Sea salt and freshly ground pepper

1 cup (2 oz/60 g) fresh bread crumbs (see Note)

2 large eggs

1 tablespoon whole or lowfat milk, if needed

PORK TATEMADO

3 lb (1.5 kg) boneless pork shoulder

2 cups (16 fl oz/500 ml) cider vinegar

6 cloves garlic, coarsely chopped

Sea salt and freshly ground pepper

4 ancho chiles *and* 8 guajillo chiles, seeded (page 108)

1 teaspoon canola oil

1 medium-large ripe tomato, cut into eighths

2 large tomatillos, husked and rinsed (page 17), then quartered

2-inch (5-cm) piece fresh ginger, peeled and chopped

½-inch (12-mm) piece true cinnamon bark or ¾ tea-spoon ground cinnamon

¼ teaspoon coriander seeds

Large pinch of dried thyme

4 whole cloves

1 lb (500 g) pork neck bones, ordered in advance from the butcher

3 bay leaves

Marinated Red Onions (page 115), finely shredded cabbage, thinly sliced radishes, and warmed corn tortillas (page 115) or White Rice (page 110) for serving

Using a sharp knife, poke holes in all sides of the pork shoulder and put into a deep bowl. Pour the vinegar into a blender, add the garlic, and process until smooth. Add 2 teaspoons sea salt and ½ teaspoon pepper, process, then pour over the meat. Turn the meat to saturate it, then cover and let marinate at room temperature for 2 hours.

Put the chiles in a bowl, add hot water to cover, weight them down with a plate, and let soak for 30 minutes. Meanwhile, in a frying pan over medium heat, heat the oil. Add the tomato and tomatillos and cook until soft and browned, about 10 minutes. Remove from the heat and let cool.

Preheat the oven to 300°F (150°C). Remove the meat from the mari-nade, reserving the marinade. Measure out ½ cup (4 fl oz/125 ml) of the marinade and place in a blender; reserve the rest. Add a third of the chiles to the blender and process until smooth. Press the mixture through a medium-mesh sieve over a large Dutch oven, discarding the solids. Repeat twice until all of the chiles are puréed and strained, adding marinade as needed for a smooth mixture. Season with sea salt. Put the ginger, cinnamon, coriander seeds, thyme, and cloves along with the cooked tomato and tomatillos into the blender. Add 1 cup (8 fl oz/250 ml) water and process until smooth. Season with sea salt, then stir into the chile mixture.

Place the meat in the Dutch oven and turn it to coat thoroughly with the chile mixture. Add the neck bones and bay leaves, cover, and place in the oven. Braise, occasionally turning the meat and checking to make sure there is still plenty of sauce in the pot (add water if necessary), until the meat is tender but not falling apart, about 2 hours. Remove from the oven. Transfer the meat to a cutting board, slice thickly, and arrange on a large platter. Pour the sauce over the slices and sprinkle with the onions, cabbage, and radishes. Serve at once, with warmed tortillas or white rice.

MAKES 6 SERVINGS

CINNAMON

In the early 1500s, the Spanish introduced to Mexico a variety of spices from the Far East—including cinnamon—which were soon used by local cooks in dozens of dishes, including *tatemado*. The name of this ancient festival dish means "something to put in fire." (It originally was cooked in a buried pot, but is now often cooked in a pot over a fire with coals on top.) The cinnamon used in *tatemado* is the deli-cately flavored true cinnamon bark native to Sri Lanka, not the stronger-tasting cassia bark from Indonesia, China, and Myanmar, which should be used in smaller amounts.

LAMB IN A SAVORY CHILE SAUCE

To make the sauce, in a blender, process the chopped onion, chiles and sauce, olive oil, tomato sauce, oregano, 2 teaspoons sea salt, and 1 teaspoon pepper until smooth.

Preheat the oven to 250°F (120°C). In a Dutch oven over medium-low heat, heat the olive oil. Stir in the sliced onions and sprinkle with sea salt and pepper. Cover and cook, stirring from time to time, until softened and light yellow, about 5 minutes. Add 1 cup (8 fl oz/ 250 ml) water and the tequila to the onions, then place the lamb on top. Spoon the sauce evenly over the lamb, cover, and place in the oven.

Bake the lamb, turning it every hour or so, until meltingly tender, 4–5 hours. The liquid should never bubble; if it does, reduce the oven temperature slightly. If the liquid is cooking away, pour ½ cup (4 fl oz/125 ml) water around the lamb.

Transfer the lamb to a cutting board and snip the strings. Cut into thick chunks and put on a warmed platter. Skim off any excess fat from the sauce and discard. Pour the sauce, along with the onions, over the lamb and garnish with the cilantro, if using. Serve at once with warm tortillas.

Serving Tips: Watercress Salad with Orange, Jicama, and Avocado (page 52) offers a nice contrast to this dish. Red Rice (page 110) could also be served alongside.

MAKES 6–8 SERVINGS

TEQUILA

Tequila is distilled from the juice of the blue agave, a plant with a pineapple-like base and long, sword-shaped branches. While tequila is best known around the world as the base for margaritas, Mexicans usually consume the spirit straight, with perhaps a bit of salt and a squeeze of lime. Always look for tequilas made from 100 percent blue agave, without additives. The most popular types are *blanco* (unaged), *reposado* (aged 2 to 12 months), and *añejo* (aged in oak barrels for over a year). The last has a mellow flavor, much like a good brandy, that complements the chipotle sauce in this recipe.

FOR THE SAUCE:

1 white onion, coarsely chopped

6 *chiles chipotles en adobo* with 2 teaspoons sauce

½ cup (4 fl oz/125 ml) olive oil

2 cups (16 fl oz/500 ml) tomato sauce

1 teaspoon dried oregano, preferably Mexican

Sea salt and freshly ground pepper

2 tablespoons olive oil

2 large white onions, sliced

Sea salt and freshly ground pepper

½ cup (4 fl oz/125 ml) tequila *añejo*

6 lb (3 kg) lamb shoulder, trimmed of excess fat, rolled, and tied

3 tablespoons chopped fresh cilantro (fresh coriander) (optional)

Corn tortillas, warmed (page 115), for serving

DESSERTS

With choices such as mango, papaya, and guava, it is little surprise that many Mexican meals end with slices of tropical fruit or a fruit ice. Traditional Spanish desserts such as flan and bread pudding are also favorites. In recent years, various chocolate cakes have been created, such as the one in this chapter with the complementary rich, fruity flavor of ancho chiles, a combination that was used in the courts of the Aztecs as a beverage.

COFFEE AND KAHLÚA FLAN

In a small, heavy saucepan over medium high-heat, combine the sugar, ¼ cup (2 fl oz/60 ml) water, and the corn syrup and bring to a boil, stirring only a few times, until the syrup is clear. Reduce the heat to medium and simmer, without stirring, until the syrup begins to darken, 10–15 minutes. Swirl the pan until the syrup is a deep amber, about 1 minute. Immediately pour the caramel into a 9-by-2-inch (23-by-5-cm) round cake pan or into 8–10 individual molds and tilt to distribute it evenly over the bottom and a little up the sides. Set aside.

Preheat the oven to 325°F (165°C). In a large saucepan over medium-low heat, combine the condensed milk, half-and-half, whole milk, and cinnamon and bring to a simmer. Remove from the heat and let steep for 10 minutes. Remove the cinnamon and stir in the Kahlúa and the diluted coffee. In a bowl, lightly whisk the eggs until blended. Gradually whisk in the warm milk mixture and then the vanilla. Strain the mixture through a fine-mesh sieve into the prepared mold(s). Place the mold(s) in a large roasting pan and put on the center rack of the oven. Pour boiling water to a depth of 1 inch (2.5 cm) into the baking pan. Bake, uncovered, until just set and a knife inserted near the center comes out clean, 1–1½ hours for the large flan, and 40–60 minutes for the individual molds. Remove the roasting pan from the oven, remove the flan(s), and transfer to a wire rack. Let cool, cover with plastic wrap, and refrigerate for at least 6 hours or for up to 2 days.

To unmold, run a thin knife around the inside edge of the mold(s). Place a serving plate with a rim over the top and invert the plate and flan together. Lift off the mold carefully, scraping out any of the remaining caramel to run over the flan and around the plate. If you have made a large flan, cut into thin wedges to serve.

MAKES 8–10 SERVINGS

CARAMELIZING SUGAR

Always use caution when caramelizing sugar, as the syrup is dangerously hot. Use a heavy, light-colored saucepan, preferably copper, so you can judge the color of the syrup. The addition of a little corn syrup helps prevent the sugar from recrystallizing on the sides of the pan. Once all the ingredients are in the pan, the sugar has dissolved, and the liquid has begun to turn amber, do not stir it. Also, never leave the stove once the syrup starts to color. The caramelizing process is quick, and the syrup can burn easily.

⅔ cup (5 oz/155 g) sugar

1 tablespoon corn syrup

1 can (14 fl oz/430 ml) sweetened condensed milk

¾ cup (6 fl oz/180 ml) half-and-half (half cream)

1 cup (8 fl oz/250 ml) whole milk

2-inch (5-cm) piece true cinnamon bark (page 85) or 1-inch (2.5-cm) piece cassia cinnamon bark

1 tablespoon Kahlúa or other coffee-flavored liqueur

2 teaspoons instant coffee granules dissolved in 1 teaspoon boiling water

5 large eggs

¾ teaspoon vanilla extract (essence)

90

BRANDY-INFUSED BREAD PUDDING

6 cups cubed day-old French bread (¾-inch/2-cm cubes)

¼ cup (2 fl oz/60 ml) canola or peanut oil

½ lb (250 g) *piloncillo (far right)*, or 1 cup (7 oz/ 220 g) firmly packed dark brown or raw sugar

½ cup (4 fl oz/125 ml) apple juice

½ cup (4 fl oz/125 ml) brandy or apple juice

4 tablespoons (2 oz/60 g) unsalted butter

4-inch (10-cm) piece true cinnamon bark (page 85) or 2-inch (5-cm) piece cassia cinnamon bark, plus 1 teaspoon ground cinnamon

3 large eggs

5 tablespoons (2½ fl oz/ 75 ml) whole milk

¼ teaspoon ground allspice

1 cup (4 oz/125 g) shredded *queso Chihuahua* (see Notes, page 44) or extra-sharp white Cheddar cheese

2 apples, peeled, cored, and chopped

½ cup (3 oz/90 g) raisins

½ cup (2 oz/60 g) pine nuts or chopped pecans, lightly toasted (page 115)

Preheat the oven to 350°F (180°C). Butter a 9-by-13-inch (23-by-33-cm) baking dish. Put the bread cubes into a bowl, add the oil, and toss to coat evenly. Spread the bread cubes on a baking sheet, place in the oven, and toast, turning occasionally to color all sides, until golden, 5–10 minutes. Remove from the oven and let cool.

In a saucepan over medium heat, combine the *piloncillo*, 2 cups (16 fl oz/500 ml) water, apple juice, and brandy and bring to a low boil, stirring until the sugar dissolves. Add 1 tablespoon of the butter and the cinnamon bark. Stir until the butter melts, and then simmer until the syrup thickens, about 5 minutes. Remove from the heat, and remove and discard the cinnamon bark. You should have at least 3 cups (24 fl oz/750 ml) syrup.

Spread half of the bread cubes over the bottom of the prepared dish. In a small bowl, whisk the eggs until blended, then whisk in the milk, ground cinnamon, and allspice. Dribble half of the egg mixture evenly over the bread. Sprinkle evenly with half of the cheese, apples, raisins, and nuts, then very slowly pour about 1½ cups (12 fl oz/375 ml) of the syrup evenly over the surface. Cut the remaining 3 tablespoons butter into small pieces and, using half of the pieces, dot the surface. Layer the remaining bread on top, dribble with the remaining egg mixture, and sprinkle with the remaining cheese, apples, raisins, and nuts. Very slowly pour the remaining syrup evenly over the surface so that all of it is absorbed into the bread. Dot with the remaining butter pieces.

Bake, uncovered, until the top is lightly browned, about 25 minutes. Remove from the oven and let cool slightly before serving.

Note: Bread pudding, or capirotada, *is a traditional Lenten dish in Mexico and would usually follow a meal of fish or vegetable fritters. It also makes a simple but filling snack when drenched with cold milk.*

MAKES 10–12 SERVINGS

PILONCILLO

Piloncillo is unrefined sugar and an everyday sweetener in Mexico. It is formed by pouring boiled sugarcane syrup into cone-, bar-, or disk-shaped molds, where it hardens into a dark brown crystallized sugar. Cones, weighing from 1 to 7 ounces (30 to 220 g), are the most common shape found outside Mexico. They can be quite hard and may need to be chopped into pieces, though they will dissolve easily in liquid. Dark brown sugar can be substituted, but it does not have the same deep flavor. Look for *piloncillo* in the ethnic food section of your market or in Mexican grocery stores.

MANGO ICE

In a saucepan over high heat, bring the sugar and 1 cup (8 fl oz/ 250 ml) water to a boil, stirring with a wooden spoon until the sugar dissolves and a light syrup forms. Remove from the heat and let cool. Cover and refrigerate until ready to use.

In a blender or food processor, purée the mango pulp until smooth. You should have about 3 cups (1½ lb/750 g). Transfer to a bowl and add the sugar syrup, orange zest, and the Cointreau, if using. Stir well. Cover and refrigerate until chilled, at least 3 hours or up to 24 hours.

Transfer the chilled mixture to an ice-cream maker and freeze according to the manufacturer's instructions. Cover and freeze until firm, at least 2 hours or up to 1 day, before serving. To serve, spoon or scoop the ice into dessert bowls and garnish with mint. Serve at once.

MAKES ABOUT 1 QT (1 L)

1 cup (8 oz/250 g) sugar

4 large, ripe mangoes, pitted and cubed *(far left),* or 1 jar (1½ lb/750 g) mangoes in light syrup, drained

Grated zest of 1 orange

1 teaspoon Cointreau or other orange-flavored liqueur (optional)

Mint sprigs for garnish

PREPARING MANGOES

To prepare a mango for use in this recipe, stand the mango on one end. With a large, sharp knife, cut down one of the flat sides, cutting around and against the pit. You should have 1 large piece. Repeat on the other side of the mango. Place each piece flesh side up and carefully score the flesh in a grid pattern just down to, but not piercing, the peel. Press against the center of the peel to invert, pushing out the scored cubes of flesh. Then, using the knife, cut the cubes away from the peel. Scrape the peel to remove any remaining flesh.

MANDARIN MOUSSE

1 can (11 oz/345 g) mandarin oranges, drained

2 large eggs, separated

6 tablespoons (3 oz/90 g) sugar

2¼ teaspoons (1 package) unflavored powdered gelatin

1 cup (8 fl oz/250 ml) heavy (double) cream, chilled

2 tablespoons Cointreau or other orange-flavored liqueur or mandarin juice

Grated zest of 2 mandarin oranges, tangerines, or oranges (page 74)

⅓ cup (1½ oz/45 g) sliced (flaked) almonds, toasted (page 115)

Finely chop the mandarin orange segments, then lay the pieces on paper towels to absorb the excess moisture. Set aside.

In a stainless-steel or other heatproof bowl, stir together the egg whites and 4 tablespoons (2 oz/60 g) of the sugar. Place over (but not touching) simmering water in a saucepan until the sugar dissolves, about 1 minute. Remove from the heat and, using an electric mixer on medium-high speed, beat until soft peaks form and the mixture is cool. Set aside. Rinse the beaters.

In a small stainless-steel bowl, stir the egg yolks with a fork until blended. Set aside. In a small saucepan over medium heat, stir together the remaining 2 tablespoons sugar and ¼ cup (2 fl oz/60 ml) water and bring to a boil. Remove from the heat, sprinkle on the gelatin, and whisk until dissolved. (It will be lumpy at first; continue whisking until smooth.) Pour the warm gelatin mixture over the egg yolks and, using the electric mixer on medium speed, beat until the mixture is cool. Set aside. Rinse the beaters.

In a large bowl, using the electric mixer on medium-high speed, beat the cream until soft peaks form. Add the Cointreau and beat for just a moment to incorporate. Fold in the egg-white mixture and then the egg-yolk mixture. Add the mandarin orange pieces and the citrus zest and fold gently to distribute evenly without deflating the mixture.

Divide the mousse among 4 or 5 individual goblets, or spoon into a single serving bowl. Cover with plastic wrap and refrigerate until ready to serve.

Just before serving, garnish the mousse with the toasted almonds.

MAKES 4 OR 5 SERVINGS

MANDARIN ORANGES
The Spanish first introduced citrus fruits in Mexico during the sixteenth century. Among the types they brought was the diminutive mandarin, which has a refreshing, somewhat bittersweet tang, as well as loose skin that makes it very easy to peel. Citrus terminology can be confusing, however. In the United States, some mandarin varieties are known as tangerines, a name that came into fashion in the nineteenth century when many mandarins were cultivated in North Africa, around the city of Tangier.

POLVORONES

In a bowl, using an electric mixer on medium speed, beat together the butter and shortening until creamy. Add 1½ cups (5 oz/150 g) of the confectioners' sugar, the orange zest, and the orange juice and beat until blended.

In another bowl, stir together the flour, nuts, and sea salt. Add the flour mixture 1 tablespoon at a time to the butter mixture, beating until thoroughly incorporated. The dough will be crumbly. Transfer the dough to a large sheet of plastic wrap and press the dough into a ball. Wrap and then refrigerate for 1–2 hours.

Position a rack in the upper third of the oven and preheat the oven to 325°F (165°C). Line a baking sheet with parchment (baking) paper or with a silicone baking mat.

Using your hands, roll small pieces of the dough into ¾-inch (2-cm) balls. Place the balls on the prepared baking sheet, spacing them about 1 inch (2.5 cm) apart and gently pressing them to flatten slightly.

Bake the cookies until the edges turn pale gold, 10–15 minutes.

Meanwhile, place the remaining 1 cup (3 oz/90 g) confectioners' sugar in a shallow bowl. When the cookies are ready, remove the baking sheet from the oven. While they are still hot, using a spatula, remove the cookies one at a time and carefully roll them in the sugar. Set aside on a rack and let cool completely, then roll them again in the sugar, shaking off any excess.

Serve the cookies at once, or layer between sheets of parchment paper in an airtight container and store at room temperature for up to 3 days.

MAKES ABOUT 3 DOZEN COOKIES

½ cup (4 oz/125 g) unsalted butter, at room temperature

½ cup (4 oz/125 g) solid vegetable shortening

2½ cups (8 oz/250 g) sifted confectioners' (icing) sugar

1 teaspoon finely grated orange zest

1 tablespoon fresh orange juice

2 cups (10 oz/315 g) unbleached all-purpose (plain) flour

⅔ cup (2½ oz/75 g) ground walnuts

¼ teaspoon sea salt

CHOCOLATE CAKE WITH ANCHO WHIPPED CREAM

Nonstick vegetable-oil cooking spray

1 tablet (3 oz/90 g) Mexican chocolate (page 27), coarsely chopped

1 cup (5½ oz/170 g) blanched almonds, toasted (page 115)

⅓ cup (1½ oz/45 g) all-purpose (plain) flour, sifted

¼ cup (¾ oz/20 g) Dutch-process cocoa powder, sifted

2 ancho chiles, seeded and toasted (page 108), then ground (page 114)

½ cup (4 oz/125 g) unsalted butter, at room temperature

1 cup (8 oz/250 g) granulated sugar

6 large eggs, separated, at room temperature

1 tablespoon Kahlúa or crème de cacao liqueur

¼ teaspoon almond extract (essence)

Pinch of sea salt

Ancho Whipped Cream (far right)

Finely grated bittersweet chocolate or chocolate curls

Preheat the oven to 350°F (180°C). Line the bottom of a 9-by-2½-inch (23-by-6-cm) springform pan with parchment (baking) paper. Lightly coat the pan sides with the cooking spray. In a food processor, combine the chocolate and almonds and pulse to grind finely. Transfer to a small bowl; add the flour, cocoa, and 1 tablespoon of the ground chiles and whisk to mix. In a large bowl, using an electric mixer on medium speed, beat the butter until pale, about 2 minutes. Reduce the speed to low and gradually add ½ cup (4 oz/125 g) of the granulated sugar, stopping the mixer at times to scrape down the bowl sides. Increase the speed to medium and beat until the mixture is light and fluffy, 3–5 minutes. Add the egg yolks one at a time, beating until the mixture is smooth, stopping to scrape down the bowl sides. With the mixer on low speed, add the ground chocolate mixture, Kahlúa, and almond extract and beat just until blended.

In a large bowl, combine the egg whites and sea salt. Using clean beaters, beat on low speed until frothy. Gradually add the remaining granulated sugar while beating constantly. Increase the speed to medium-high and beat until the whites form stiff, glossy peaks, about 2 minutes. Using a large rubber spatula, gently fold a third of the whites into the batter. Fold in the remaining whites in 2 batches just until combined. Transfer the batter to the prepared pan and smooth the surface. Place the pan on a baking sheet to catch any drips. Bake the cake until a toothpick comes out clean, 40–45 minutes. Transfer the cake to a wire rack and let cool for 15 minutes. Release the sides of the pan and lift off. Place a wire rack on top of the cake and invert the cake and rack together. Lift off the pan bottom and paper and let cool completely.

Whisk the ancho whipped cream until thick enough to hold its shape. Place the cake, bottom side up, on a serving plate and coat with a thick layer of the cream. Top with grated chocolate and serve.

MAKES 10–12 SERVINGS

ANCHO WHIPPED CREAM

In a small bowl, whisk together ⅓ cup (3 fl oz/80 ml) heavy (double) cream and 1 teaspoon of the ground ancho chile powder. Let stand for up to 5 minutes. Whisk again and pour into a chilled large bowl. Add 1¼ cups (10 fl oz/310 ml) more cream and 1 tablespoon vanilla extract (essence) and, using an electric mixer on low speed, beat until the cream thickens. Increase the speed to medium-high and beat until soft peaks form. Reduce the speed to medium and gradually add 3 tablespoons sifted confectioners' (icing) sugar, beating until soft mounds form.

RUM-RAISIN CHEESECAKE

To make the crust, in a bowl, stir together the crushed gingersnaps and butter until the crumbs are evenly moistened. Transfer the crumbs to a 9-by-2½-inch (23-by-6-cm) springform pan and press evenly onto the bottom and 1 inch (2.5 cm) up the sides to form a thin, even crust. Refrigerate for 30 minutes.

Preheat the oven to 350°F (180°C). Put the raisins in a small saucepan, add the rum, and heat over medium heat until the raisins are plump and soft, about 10 minutes. Remove from the heat and set aside.

In a bowl, using an electric mixer on medium speed, beat the cream cheese until smooth. Add ¾ cup (6 oz/185 g) of the sugar and 1 teaspoon of the vanilla and beat until blended. Add the eggs one at a time, beating just until smooth after each addition and stopping to scrape down the sides and along the bottom of the bowl so that the ingredients are thoroughly mixed. Add the raisins and rum and the orange zest and beat just until well mixed. Pour the filling into the prepared crust. Bake until firm, 50–60 minutes. Remove the cheesecake from the oven and immediately place in the refrigerator on a kitchen towel to chill for 15 minutes. Raise the oven temperature to 450°F (230°C).

In a bowl, stir together the sour cream, the remaining ¼ cup (2 oz/65 g) sugar, and the remaining 2 teaspoons vanilla. Remove the cheesecake from the refrigerator, pour the sour cream mixture evenly over the top, and return the cheesecake to the oven to bake for 10 minutes. Transfer to a wire rack and let cool completely, then cover and refrigerate until well chilled, at least 24 hours or for up to 3 days. To serve, release the sides of the springform pan and lift off; leave the cake on the pan bottom. Transfer the cake to a serving plate. Serve cold or at room temperature.

MAKES 12 SERVINGS

FOR THE CRUST:

1½ cups (4½ oz/140 g) finely crushed gingersnaps (about 36)

4 tablespoons (2 oz/60 g) unsalted butter, melted

½ cup (3 oz/90 g) raisins

¼ cup (2 fl oz/60 ml) dark rum

1½ lb (750 g) cream cheese, at room temperature

1 cup (8 oz/250 g) sugar

3 teaspoons vanilla extract (essence)

3 large eggs

1 teaspoon finely grated orange zest

2 cups (16 oz/500 g) sour cream

MEXICAN VANILLA

The Totonaco people of Veracruz were the first to ferment and dry the vanilla bean, the seed-pod of a climbing orchid native to Mexico. Vanilla is now grown in many tropical parts of the world, with Madagascar the top producer. True Mexican vanilla, which is deeply flavored and richly scented, is highly prized.

In the past, however, some unscrupulous producers created a serious scare by marketing imitation vanilla that contained coumarin, a highly toxic substance. Always seek out products labeled "pure vanilla extract" from the Papantla region, in the state of Veracruz, for the finest Mexican product.

MEXICAN BASICS

Mexican food is true fusion cuisine. When the indigenous peoples merged their trio of essential ingredients— corn, beans, and tomatoes—and their flavorings—chocolate, vanilla, and, of course, chiles—with the wheat, meats, rice, citrus fruits, and spices introduced by the Spanish, one of the world's most popular and exciting cuisines was born. The following information will help you to re-create Mexico's traditional dishes in your own kitchen.

REGIONAL TRADITIONS

The foods of Mexico, like the land itself, are diverse. This vast country— more than 2,000 miles (3,400 km) from top to bottom, and just about that wide on its northern border— embraces expansive stretches of desert, high mountain ranges, verdant seaside plains, steaming jungles, and fertile plateaus surrounded by forested hillsides. Slow-moving rivers snake their way through swamps of mangroves, while numerous lakes and more than 6,000 miles (9,900 km) of coastal waters bordering the Pacific Ocean and the Gulf of Mexico teem with fish and shellfish. Each of these terrains has vastly different-

plants and animals, and in each are people with varied cultural histories and cuisines.

In general, the northern border states are considered cattle country, with simple grilled meats, red beans, flour tortillas, and lots of cheese and other dairy products. In central Mexico, the foods are more complex. Even in the years before the Spanish conquest, the ancient cities of Teotihuacán and Tenochtitlán (now Mexico City) were the center of major trade routes, and exotic foods from distant regions of the country were often used in the preparation of local dishes.

With the arrival of the Spanish (especially the convent nuns of Puebla), elaborate dishes such as Mole Poblano (page 26) and Stuffed Poblano Chiles with Walnut Sauce (page 18) were created—dishes that have earned a place at the nucleus of Mexico's cuisine. The Spanish, after 300 years of Moorish domination, were themselves influenced by North African culinary traditions, including the use of such ingredients as citrus fruits and rice. When the Spanish came to Mexico, they brought some of their adopted foods along with them.

In time, these new items became part of Mexico's culinary heritage as well.

Seafood is the food of choice on both coasts, but it is in Veracruz on the Gulf of Mexico where it is served with the most gusto and variety. Much of the influence here is from the Caribbean, with a strong Spanish touch. Capers and olives are as much at home in local dishes as chiles are, and all three can be found in Veracruz-Style Red Snapper (page 25).

The foods of the three states that make up the Yucatán peninsula, that flat thumb of land jutting out between the Gulf of Mexico and the Caribbean, strongly reflect the Mayan past of its indigenous peoples, making this a cuisine very different from those of other regions. The Mayan practices of flavoring dishes such as chicken or pork with *achiote* (page 113) and cooking them underground as in Pibil-Style Baked Chicken (page 66) remain virtually unchanged today.

INGREDIENTS

In a country of such diverse regions and culinary traditions, there is almost no limit to the variety of ingredients found in local kitchens. If you are fortunate to be able to visit and shop in a market in Mexico, some still in the same locations they occupied thousands of years ago, you will be overwhelmed by the abundance of fruits, vegetables, chiles, herbs, and spices. This is truly one-stop shopping, with vendors offering everything from live turkeys, freshly made cheeses, and sea salt to colorful oilcloth for covering your table. But just because you find a ripe, ready-to-eat papaya or mango one day, do not expect to find the same fruit on the next. The markets in Mexico reflect the seasons.

More and more of the supermarkets in the United States are carrying fresh ingredients used in Mexican cooking, especially chiles, tomatillos, and jicama. If your market does not have them, just ask, as they are available and can be ordered. For other ingredients, check out the Mexican grocery stores in your area, or search for Internet or mail-order sources. Following is a discussion of the four most basic ingredients in Mexican cooking.

CHILES

When most people think about Mexican food, it is the fiery chile that first comes to mind. Seldom does a dish arrive at the table without having chiles in it or without a chile-infused salsa served alongside. Chiles, either fresh or dried, are indispensable ingredients in almost all dishes except sweets and desserts—and even occasionally show up in them, too.

While all chiles have some degree of pungency, this varies tremendously, just as there is a broad range of flavor differences. With the exception of the small jalapeños and serranos, do not try to substitute one chile for another, or you will come up with a completely different-tasting dish. These two chiles do differ, with the serrano having a grassier flavor, but they can usually be interchanged satisfactorily.

A large selection of fresh chiles is now available at most supermarkets. The jalapeño and serrano are usually chopped and used in salsas or pickled whole, and the larger jalapeños are sometimes stuffed. But it is the big, pudgy poblano that is most often stuffed for *chiles rellenos* (see the recipe on page 18 for Stuffed Poblano Chiles with Walnut Sauce, a well-known version of the dish). The poblano is also frequently roasted and cut into strips, or *rajas*, and used as a condiment or as a topping.

Sometimes fresh chiles are roasted and seeded, then stuffed, sliced, or chopped. Shown opposite are the steps for roasting and seeding them. For more information on handling fresh chiles, see page 39.

1 Roasting fresh chiles: Using tongs, place the chiles directly in or over the high flame of a gas stove and turn often until the skin is charred and blistered, 2–3 minutes. Or roast the chiles over the very hot fire of a charcoal or gas grill for 3–5 minutes, placing them as close to the fire as possible. Alternatively, broil (grill) the chiles on an aluminum foil–lined pan, placing them as close to the heat source as possible and turning them often, until blackened, 5–10 minutes. (Broiled chiles will be too soft to stuff but can be used for other recipes.)

2 Steaming the chiles: After roasting, place the chiles in a paper or heavy-duty plastic bag and let sweat for about 8 minutes to help loosen the skin. This will also soften the flesh, so do not leave them too long.

3 Removing the skin: Pick and peel away as much skin as possible. Do not worry if some charred bits remain.

4 Seeding the chiles: For stuffing (shown here), using a small knife, slit each chile lengthwise from the stem area to the bottom, leaving ½ inch (12 mm) uncut on top and at least ¼ inch (6 mm) on the bottom. Leaving the stem intact, remove the seeds and membranes with your fingers. Wipe the inside of the chile with a damp towel, checking to see that all the seeds and membranes are removed. Dry well. For slicing or chopping, slit the chile lengthwise and spread it out. Cut out the stem, then remove the seeds and membranes.

Purchasing dried chiles can be confusing, as they are sometimes mislabeled in the market, but again, each variety has a distinct taste and the chiles cannot be used interchangeably. Some dried chiles, such as the ancho, can be stuffed, but most are used in salsas or as an integral part of a dish such as a mole. Ancho, mulato, and pasilla chiles are used in traditional Mole Poblano (page 26), and the distinct flavor of the guajillo is found in many stewlike dishes, including Pork Tatemado (page 85). Some of the very hot dried chiles, such as the árbol, are toasted and ground for use as chile powder. One of the most popular of all dried chiles is the chipotle, the smoked and dried jalapeño. This chile is most commonly pickled or prepared in an adobo sauce (see page 77), and many dishes benefit from its rich flavor.

To seed dried chiles, wipe them with a damp cloth, then slit them lengthwise and use a small, sharp knife to remove the seeds.

To toast dried chiles, clean them with a damp cloth, then heat a *comal*, griddle, or heavy frying pan over medium heat. Add the whole or seeded chile, press down firmly for a few seconds with a spatula, turn the chile, and press down for just a few seconds more before removing. The chile should change color slightly and start to give off its aroma.

CORN

Throughout Mexico, corn is the most common culinary element. Corn *masa* (page 35) is the fundamental ingredient in corn tortillas, which are the bread, the plate, and the spoon of Mexican cuisine. They are also wrapped around tasty bites of food to make tacos, folded over cheese for quesadillas, or fashioned into enchiladas. Corn *masa* is patted and pinched into various shapes, too, and, depending on the region, turned into *flautas* (page 39) and other *antojitos* (little bites and snacks). Nor can we forget the part *masa* plays in tamales (page 20), which are on the menu at almost every special occasion in Mexico.

TOMATOES

The tomato has been an essential ingredient in Mexican cuisine since pre-Columbian times. Cooks rely on vine-ripened, sweet, deep red tomatoes and, unless used fresh, usually roast them before using. To roast tomatoes, line a heavy frying pan with heavy-duty aluminum foil and heat over medium heat. Roast the tomatoes, turning them occasionally, until the skins are blackened and the interiors soften. The most blackened skin may be removed before using.

BEANS

Seldom a day goes by that protein-rich beans are not eaten in one form or another in Mexican households. Through the ages, it has been these humble legumes that, along with the corn in *masa,* have provided the fundamental nourishment for the Mexican people. Black beans are cooked in the southern regions, while pinto beans are customary in the north, but myriad other varieties are cooked throughout the country as well. For two basic bean dishes to serve alongside the recipes in this book, or on their own sprinkled with a little cheese, see page 111.

TECHNIQUES AND EQUIPMENT

It is truly the sauce that defines the dish in Mexican cuisine—not bland flour-thickened sauces, but aromatic ones with an abundance of flavor that captivates the senses. If a dish is not made with a seed- or nut-based sauce such as a mole or *pipián,* it will be cloaked with a robust tomato sauce. Even a plain piece of grilled meat will be accompanied with a table salsa. And the framework for all of these will be not only the ingredients but also the techniques and equipment used to prepare them.

There are a few essential techniques in Mexican cuisine: roasting, toasting, and searing. All three are designed to bring out the full flavor of the ingredients on which they are used.

Whether tomatoes, tomatillos, chiles, onions, or garlic, roasting—or briefly bringing ingredients in contact with high heat—causes the flavors of the ingredient to take on a smoky character. Roasting is achieved by directly exposing an ingredient to a heat source, as with roasting chiles over a gas flame on the stove top, or by using a *comal*, griddle, or heavy frying pan, as with garlic, onions, and tomatoes.

Spices are almost always toasted briefly while whole and then ground, while nuts are toasted before chopping. The depth of flavor of dried chiles is also intensified when lightly toasted. To toast these ingredients, use a *comal*, griddle, or frying pan.

The first step to making most cooked Mexican sauces is to bring the puréed mixture into contact with a hot oil-coated surface. This searing concentrates and melds the often harsh and disparate flavors of the ingredients into a robust, earthy blend. It also helps to thicken the sauce and deepen its color. Traditional Mexican cooks use an earthenware *cazuela* (page 113) for cooking these sauces, but you can substitute a heavy-bottomed metal pot. A cast-iron Dutch oven (preferably enamel-coated) is an especially good choice, as it has deep sides to contain any splatters when the purée first hits the hot surface and it retains heat well.

Following are some other tools you will need to prepare many of the dishes in this book.

The blender has become one of the most important cooking utensils in the Mexican kitchen. It is indispensable for making sauces and has replaced the traditional *molcajete*, or basalt mortar (page 115), in all but the most rural areas. A *molcajete* is still an important tool for making chunky sauces, such as salsas and guacamole, or for grinding small amounts of spices and seeds. Considerable time is saved by using a blender for smooth sauces, however. A food processor is not recommended for blending or puréeing the sauces in this book, as it will not completely purée the tougher ingredients such as nuts and dried-chile skins. A selection of sieves, including medium- and fine-mesh types, is ideal for straining blended sauces. When straining a sauce, use the back of a large spoon, if necessary, to push the sauce through the sieve.

Similarly, an electric spice or small coffee grinder (page 114) is an excellent time-saving device. This tool makes quick work of grinding the whole spices and seeds essential in Mexican cooking.

One of the most frequently used utensils in the Mexican kitchen is a metal or clay *comal* (page 114). A cast-iron griddle or heavy cast-iron frying pan may be substituted. Perfect for roasting and toasting ingredients, this tool is also essential for making or warming tortillas.

Authentic tamales steamers can be purchased in most Mexican grocery stores, but any big pot with a tight lid will work. You will also need a steamer basket or a perforated rack that can be propped up at least 3 inches (7.5 cm) above the bottom of the pan (see page 21). Specialized Mexican steamers have an opening with a spout in the lower section, so that additional water can be poured into the pot.

While Mexican food can be served in most any type of dinnerware, to do it justice, search out colorful Talavera serving dishes and table settings if price is no object. For more affordable substitutes, check your local Mexican markets or other stores.

BASIC RECIPES

Here are some of the basic recipes referred to throughout this book.

WHITE RICE

2 tablespoons canola or safflower oil

1½ cups (10½ oz/330 g) long-grain white rice

¼ white onion, sliced or chopped

2 cloves garlic, minced

2½ cups (20 fl oz/625 ml) chicken stock *(this page, far right),* prepared low-sodium broth, or water

1 bay leaf

Sea salt

2 serrano or jalapeño chiles (optional)

In a heavy saucepan over medium heat, heat the oil. When hot, add the rice and stir with a wooden spoon until the rice is chalky white and speckled with tan, 7–8 minutes. You will hear the sounds of dry cracking as the rice is cooking.

Add the onion and garlic, stir, and cook for about 1 minute. Add the stock, bay leaf, scant 1 teaspoon sea salt, and the whole chiles, if using. Raise the heat to high, bring to a boil, reduce the heat to medium, and cook for 4 minutes, stirring occasionally. Cover, reduce the heat to very low, and simmer until all the liquid is absorbed, about 15 minutes longer.

Remove from the heat and let stand, covered, for 10 minutes. Before serving, remove the bay leaf and chiles and fluff the rice with a fork. Makes 5 or 6 servings.

RED RICE

1 can (14½ oz/455 g) whole tomatoes, drained

3 tablespoons chopped white onion

2 small cloves garlic

¼ cup (2 fl oz/60 ml) corn or sunflower oil

1 cup (7 oz/220 g) medium-grain white rice

⅓ cup (2 oz/60 g) *each* fresh or frozen peas, fresh or frozen corn kernels, and diced peeled carrot

3 serrano chiles, slit down one side

6 fresh cilantro (fresh coriander) sprigs, tied together

Sea salt

Put the tomatoes, onion, and garlic in a blender and process until smooth. Set aside. In a saucepan over medium-high heat, heat the oil. When hot, add the rice and stir until it just starts to change color, about 1 minute. Do not allow it to brown. Add the tomato mixture and stir gently to blend. Add 2 cups (16 fl oz/500 ml) hot water, the peas, corn, carrot, chiles, cilantro, and 1½ teaspoons sea salt. Bring to a boil, shaking the pan to mix the ingredients. Reduce the heat to low. Taste the broth and add more sea salt if needed, then cover and cook for about 10 minutes.

Uncover and stir carefully so that all of the broth is mixed in (most will have been absorbed). Re-cover and cook until all the broth is absorbed, about 10 minutes longer. Remove from the heat and let stand, covered, for 10 minutes. Before serving, remove the cilantro and chiles and fluff the rice with a fork. Makes 4–6 servings.

CHICKEN, TURKEY, OR BEEF STOCK

2 lb (1 kg) chicken or turkey bones, wings, necks, or other parts, or 2 lb (1 kg) beef bones (preferably with marrow)

1 white onion, quartered

1 celery stalk with leaves

3 cloves garlic

10 peppercorns

2 bay leaves

Sea salt

Put the bones and/or other parts in a large pot and add 3 qt (3 l) water. Add the onion, celery, and garlic. Bring to a boil over medium-high heat, skimming off any foam from the surface. Add the peppercorns and bay leaves, reduce the heat to low, cover partially, and simmer for 3–4 hours. If too much liquid boils away, add 1 cup (8 fl oz/250 ml) water or as needed to end up with 1½–2 qt (1½–2 l) stock. Keep tasting, and when the flavor seems just right, add sea salt to taste, simmer a bit longer, and then remove from the heat. Let cool, then strain the stock through a fine-mesh sieve into a clean container. Cover and refrigerate overnight. The next day, using a large spoon, remove and discard the hardened fat from the surface.

Cover and refrigerate the stock for up to 3 days, or pour into airtight containers or zippered plastic freezer bags and freeze for up to 3 months. Makes 1½–2 qt (1½–2 l).

POT BEANS

1 lb (500 g) dried black or pinto beans

2 tablespoons fresh pork lard (page 114), rendered bacon fat, or canola oil

½ white onion, coarsely chopped

2 fresh epazote sprigs, if cooking black beans, or fresh cilantro (fresh coriander) sprigs

Sea salt

3 oz (90 g) *queso fresco* or feta cheese, crumbled, for serving (optional)

Pick over and rinse the beans, discarding any broken beans or grit. Transfer the beans to a pot and add water to cover by 3–4 inches (7.5–10 cm). Bring to a gentle boil over medium-high heat, reduce the heat to medium-low, and allow to simmer.

Meanwhile, in a small frying pan over medium heat, melt the lard or fat or heat the oil. Add the onion and sauté until browned, about 8 minutes. Add to the beans, scraping in all of the melted fat. Cover partially and cook the beans until they are just tender, 2–3 hours, stirring occasionally and adding water if necessary to maintain the level of water well above the beans. Add the epazote, if using black beans, or cilantro and 1½ teaspoons sea salt and continue to cook until the beans are very soft, 40–60 minutes longer.

The beans will keep, covered, in the refrigerator for up to 4 days. If serving the beans as they are, ladle the broth and beans into bowls and garnish with the cheese, if using, or use in other recipes. Makes 6 servings, with leftovers.

REFRIED BEANS

½ cup (4 oz/125 g) fresh pork lard (page 114) or ½ cup (4 fl oz/125 ml) canola or safflower oil

½ white onion, finely chopped

4 cups (28 oz/875 g) Pot Beans *(left)* with 2 cups (16 fl oz/500 ml) broth (see Notes)

Sea salt

3 oz (90 g) *queso fresco* or feta cheese, crumbled, for serving (optional)

Fried tortilla strips or chips (page 10, optional)

In a large, heavy frying pan over medium heat, melt the lard or heat the oil. Add the onion and sauté, stirring frequently, until golden and soft, about 5 minutes.

Pour in 1 cup (7 oz/220 g) of the beans with some of the broth, smashing them down with a potato masher or the back of a large spoon. Continue until all of the beans and their broth have been added and mashed. Raise the heat to medium-high and cook until the beans begin to dry out, about 10 minutes. Taste and add sea salt, if needed.

Transfer to a warmed platter or individual plates and sprinkle with the cheese, if using. If desired, serve the fried tortilla strips alongside for scooping up the beans. Makes 4–6 servings.

Notes: Frijoles refritos, *commonly called refried beans in the United States, are more accurately translated as "well-fried" beans. They can also be made with canned beans. Drain and rinse the canned beans and substitute water for the bean broth.*

SALSA VERDE

12 tomatillos, about 1 lb (500 g) total weight, husked and rinsed (page 17)

4 serrano or 2 jalapeño chiles

2 cloves garlic

Sea salt

½ cup (2½ oz/75 g) finely chopped white onion

2 tablespoons minced fresh cilantro (fresh coriander)

Put the tomatillos and chiles in a saucepan over medium heat and add water to cover. Bring to a simmer and cook, uncovered, until the tomatillos are soft, about 15 minutes.

Drain, reserving some of the liquid, and transfer to a blender. Add the garlic and process briefly until thinned but still coarse. It may be necessary to add up to ½ cup (4 fl oz/125 ml) of the reserved liquid. Pour into a small serving bowl and stir in ½ teaspoon sea salt or to taste.

Just before serving, stir in the onion and cilantro. Makes about 2½ cups (20 fl oz/625 ml).

Make-Ahead Tip: This salsa can be stored, covered, in the refrigerator for up to 2 days. If it thickens too much, stir in a spoonful or so of water.

GLOSSARY

Many areas in the United States, and in some other countries, are home to growing Mexican communities and have ethnic grocery stores or mainstream supermarkets that cater to a diversity of customers and cooking styles. If you do not live in an area where Mexican foodstuffs are readily available, look to specialty-food stores, mail-order retailers, and the Internet as good sources for authentic Mexican ingredients.

ACHIOTE PASTE This deep orange paste is made from the hard seeds of the tropical annatto tree. The seeds are ground with spices and mixed with garlic and vinegar or the juice of bitter oranges. The paste is popular in the kitchens of the Yucatán peninsula. Look for it in Mexican markets. Once opened, store tightly capped in the refrigerator.

ACITRÓN This mildly sweet, crystallized form of the biznaga cactus can be found in some Mexican markets. Candied pineapple may be substituted.

BAY LEAVES The bay leaves used in Mexican cooking are similar to those of the California laurel. Often used together with marjoram and thyme, bay leaves are sold in bundles in Mexican markets as *hierbas de olores*.

BITTER ORANGE A citrus fruit that grows in parts of Mexico, the bitter orange is used widely in the cooking of the Yucatán peninsula. Squat in shape, it has a very rough skin and is used for its juice, not for eating. The flavor is quite acidic. Bitter oranges are occasionally found in Latin American markets, especially in Texas, California, and Arizona, where they grow easily. If a recipe calls for bitter orange juice and you do not have access to the fruit, you may use a substitute made from other citrus juices: In a bowl, stir together 2 tablespoons fresh orange juice, 2 tablespoons fresh grapefruit juice, and 4 teaspoons fresh lime juice. Use at once, or cover and refrigerate for up to 2 days, although the taste diminishes.

CAZUELA This hefty, wide earthenware pot heats slowly and evenly and retains heat well, making it ideal for cooking and serving dishes such as Meatballs in Chipotle Sauce (page 82). If you have an electric stove, you may want to use a heat diffuser—a metal disk that sits between the burner and the pot—to protect the *cazuela* from the heat's intensity. Always cure a new *cazuela* before using it: Wash the *cazuela* well, then rub the exterior with the cut sides of a large, halved garlic clove. Fill with water, bring to a boil over medium heat, and simmer for 30 minutes. Repeat one more time. If the *cazuela* is not used every month or so, repeat the curing process before using.

Finally, always transfer foods cooked in a *cazuela* to another container for storage.

CHICKEN, POACHED To make the poached chicken called for in recipes in this book, put 2 lb (1 kg) chicken breasts or thighs in a saucepan, add boiling water to cover, and place over medium-high heat until the water returns to a boil, skimming off any foam that forms on the surface. Reduce the heat to medium-low and add a slice of white onion, 4 peppercorns, and 1 clove garlic. Cover and simmer until the meat is opaque throughout, about 20 minutes. Add sea salt to taste during the last 5 minutes.

CHILE POWDER Finely ground dried chiles, chile powder is not to be mistaken for the commercial spice blend known as chili powder, which usually combines ground dried chiles, cumin, oregano, and other seasonings and is used to flavor the well-known American Southwest stew of the same name. Pure chile powder, whether made from ancho or another chile variety, can be found in well-stocked markets and Mexican grocery stores, or you can make your own.

CHILES, DRIED Following are the dried chiles used in this book. For information on seeding and toasting dried chiles, see page 108.

Ancho: See page 14.

Árbol: A small, thin, reddish orange chile about 3 inches (7.5 cm) long and with smooth skin. These chiles are extremely *picante* and are used in table salsas.

Chipotle: See page 82.

Guajillo: A widely used long, pointed, brownish red chile with smooth skin. Its heat level varies from medium-hot to hot, and it has a sharp flavor.

Mulato: Similar to the ancho chile, only a darker brownish black. It has a full, chocolaty flavor, medium to mild heat, and wrinkled skin.

Pasilla: This shiny, narrow, wrinkled chile is about 6 inches (15 cm) long and has a blunt end. It is brownish black, has a complex flavor, and is usually quite hot.

CHILES, FRESH Following are descriptions of the fresh chiles used in this book. For information on handling fresh chiles, see page 39. For information on roasting and seeding fresh chiles, see page 106.

Güero: Any light-skinned chile, usually pale yellow or "blond," about 4 inches (10 cm) long, 1 inch (2.5 cm) wide, and pointed at the end. It can be quite hot.

Habanero: A small green, yellow, or orange lantern-shaped chile that is extremely hot, with a distinctive fruity flavor.

Jalapeño: A dark green, fat chile that is usually about 2 inches (5 cm) long. It can be very hot.

Poblano: Named for the state of Puebla, the poblano is a polished deep green, tapered chile with broad shoulders. Poblano chiles are about 5 inches (13 cm) long and are moderately hot.

Serrano: A small, slender, shiny chile that is very hot, with a bright acidic flavor. It is available both in green and a ripened red.

CHILES, GRINDING DRIED To grind dried chiles, first seed and toast them (page 108). Grind the toasted chiles into a fine powder in a spice grinder or in a mortar, and then pass through a fine-mesh sieve.

CILANTRO Introduced by the Spanish, this herb has become one of the signature seasonings of Mexico. The fresh green leaves resemble those of Italian (flat-leaf) parsley, but their pungent aniselike aroma and bright astringent taste are distinctive. Use it sparingly at first until you are familiar with its flavor. Look for sprigs with the smallest leaves for the cleanest flavor. It is also known as fresh coriander and Chinese parsley.

CINNAMON BARK, TRUE See page 85.

COMAL A flat, round griddle that is traditionally made of earthenware but also of cast iron or other metals. It is used to cook or warm tortillas, to toast seeds or dried chiles, or to roast garlic, onions, or tomatoes. A *comal* may be purchased in some Mexican markets.

CREMA See page 51.

CUMIN The seeds of a member of the parsley family, cumin has a sharp flavor. The whole seeds, freshly ground, are often used with garlic and other spices.

EPAZOTE See page 44.

GRINDER, SPICE An electric countertop spice or small coffee grinder reserved for spices is handy not only for quickly grinding spices, but also chiles, seeds, and nuts—an essential step in many Mexican recipes. Freshly ground spices and other ingredients will boast a fuller flavor, so grind them just before use.

JICAMA See page 52.

LARD, PORK Rendered pork fat, or lard, lends a rich taste to many Mexican dishes, including tamales (page 20) and Refried Beans (page 111). Commercially packaged lard is available, but home-made lard is more flavorful. To make your own: Cut 1 lb (500 g) good-quality pork fat into small cubes, or use a food processor to chop even finer. Preheat the oven to 300°F (150°C). Put the fat in a large, heavy pan, preferably cast iron, and place in the oven. As it melts, pour off the melted fat through a medium-mesh sieve into a heatproof container. Continue cooking until most of the fat has melted and only light golden crisp bits remain, 30–45 minutes. Cover and store in the refrigerator for up to several months. Note: rendered lard has half the cholesterol of butter.

MASA See page 35.

MOLCAJETE This three-legged basalt mortar, along with its accompanying *tejolote* (pestle), is used for grinding ingredients and making sauces, especially salsas and guacamole. *Molcajetes* can be found in many Mexican markets or by mail order through specialty-cookware stores. Look for a dark gray or black mortar with small pores, so liquid won't leak out. To prepare the *molcajete* for use, toss in a handful of uncooked rice and grind to a powder. Repeat until no tiny pieces of grit from the stone are present, usually 4–6 times. Rinse well.

NUTS, TOASTING To toast pine nuts, chopped pecans, and sliced or blanched almonds, preheat the oven to 275°F (135°C). Spread the nuts out in a small shallow pan and toast in the oven until fragrant and beginning to color, 5–10 minutes. Remove from the oven, transfer to a plate, and let cool.

ONIONS, MARINATED RED These onions are a tasty garnish for many Mexican dishes. In a heatproof bowl, combine 2 large red onions, thinly sliced or chopped, with boiling water to cover. Let soak until the onions just begin to lose some of their crispness, about 2 minutes. Drain well and return to the bowl. Add 3 tablespoons fresh bitter orange juice (page 113) or fresh lime juice; 1 habanero chile, roasted and seeded (page 106), then finely chopped; 1½ teaspoons sea salt, and a pinch of dried oregano. Marinate at room temperature for 1–2 hours, tossing occasionally, then cover and refrigerate until needed or for up to several weeks.

ONIONS, WHITE Most Mexican cooks use the common white-skinned onion, which has a clear, pungent flavor that is enhanced by roasting (page 65).

OREGANO There are more than thirteen varieties of plants called oregano growing in Mexico, but the most common variety, *Lippia graveolens* from the verbena family, is the one often labeled "Mexican oregano." It has a more pronounced flavor than Mediterranean varieties and can be found in Mexican markets and in many supermarkets.

PLANTAIN Closely related to the banana, the large, three-sided plantain is starchier and firmer. It is always cooked before eating. When ripe, fresh plantains have almost uniformly black skins and will yield to gentle finger pressure.

PUMPKIN SEEDS Seeds, especially pumpkin, have been a part of Mexican cooking since pre-Columbian times, both as thickeners and for flavor. Raw, hulled green pumpkin seeds can be found in natural-foods stores and in many supermarkets. They are always toasted before using.

QUESO FRESCO Meaning "fresh cheese" in Spanish, *queso fresco* is a soft, tangy, lightly salted cow's milk cheese that is crumbled or sliced before adding to dishes. Mild feta cheese may be substituted, but it should be rinsed first to remove excess salt.

SALT, SEA The more pronounced flavor of sea salt is ideal for cooking Mexican food. If substituting kosher salt, a bit more may have to be added. If a recipe involves a long cooking process, such as simmering beans or soup, always add salt at the end of the cooking, because the flavor will become concentrated as the liquid reduces.

TOMATILLOS See page 17.

TORTILLA PRESS Hinged metal tortilla presses can be found in Mexican groceries and specialty-cookware stores and catalogs. Look for heavy cast-iron, 6-inch (15-cm) presses with an ⅛ inch (3 mm) clearance between the plates on the hinge side. Avoid the lighter aluminum presses, which are not as efficient and are easily broken.

TORTILLAS, WARMING To warm tortillas to serve as an accompaniment to many Mexican dishes, wrap stacks of 5 tortillas each in aluminum foil and warm in a 275°F (135°C) oven for 5–10 minutes. To heat fewer tortillas, put them, one at a time, on a *comal*, griddle, or frying pan over low heat, and warm for several seconds on each side.

INDEX

SIMON & SCHUSTER SOURCE
A Division of Simon & Schuster, Inc.
Rockefeller Center
1230 Avenue of the Americas
New York, NY 10020

WILLIAMS-SONOMA
Founder and Vice-Chairman: Chuck Williams

WELDON OWEN INC.
Chief Executive Officer: John Owen
President: Terry Newell
Chief Operating Officer: Larry Partington
Vice President, International Sales: Stuart Laurence
Creative Director: Gaye Allen
Series Editor: Sarah Putman Clegg
Editor: Heather Belt
Designer: Teri Gardiner
Production Director: Chris Hemesath
Color Manager: Teri Bell
Shipping and Production Coordinator: Libby Temple

Weldon Owen wishes to thank the following
people for their generous assistance and support
in producing this book: Copy Editor Sharon Silva;
Consulting Editor Carolyn Miller; Food Stylists
Kim Konecny and Erin Quon; Photographer's Assistant
Faiza Ali; Proofreaders Desne Ahlers and Arin Hailey;
and Indexer Ken DellaPenta.

Set in Trajan, Utopia, and Vectora.

Williams-Sonoma Collection *Mexican* was
conceived and produced by Weldon Owen Inc.,
814 Montgomery Street, San Francisco,
California 94133, in collaboration with
Williams-Sonoma, 3250 Van Ness Avenue,
San Francisco, California 94109.

A Weldon Owen Production
Copyright © 2003 by Weldon Owen Inc. and
Williams-Sonoma Inc.

For information regarding special discounts for
bulk purchases, please contact Simon & Schuster
Special Sales at 1-800-456-6798 or
business@simonandschuster.com

Color separations by Bright Arts Graphics
Singapore (Pte.) Ltd.
Printed and bound in Singapore by Tien Wah
Press (Pte.) Ltd.

First printed in 2003.

10 9 8 7 6 5

Library of Congress Cataloging-in-Publication
data is available.

ISBN 0-7432-5334-5

A NOTE ON WEIGHTS AND MEASURES

All recipes include customary U.S. and metric measurements. Metric conversions are based on
a standard developed for these books and have been rounded off. Actual weights may vary.